Lowercase is always used in the name "satan" out of disrespect.

Thanks to Julie Wendover and Tina Meehan for proofreading!
Cover design by Rachel Chahanovich

Contents

Introduction

Truth Matters

After nearly forty years in Christian ministry, I have never seen a spirit of confusion and deception, like that which has been released in the church today. The Apostle Paul warned us that a time would come when Christians would be unable to digest sound teaching but would instead crave messages that feel good and confirm their own agenda.[1] There is no longer any doubt that this day has come and it is all the more reason we should be diligent to study what is being presented and not merely accept what is popular. The Bible tells us that the Bereans were noble minded and though they received the word with eagerness, they examined the Scriptures daily to see if the things being said were true.[2] They didn't check their brains at the door and neither can we. They were able to receive the power and presence of the Holy Spirit as well as the restoration of His truth to the church. They were truly spiritual. Today however, many have accepted the notion that being spiritual or loving is to be accepting of another preacher's position as a "unique perspective" regardless of whether it is Biblical. This kind of love and acceptance looks good and even godly on the surface, but is it really love or fear of man or even worse a Universalist spirit? No one in their right mind seeks confrontation, yet true love and friendship often demand it. That is why we must speak the truth in love[3] and not what is popular or accepted. The love chapter is clear that true godly love does not rejoice with unrighteousness but only with the truth.[4] Of course, the truth must be presented in love and not in judgment, but where is the love in allowing or

---

[1] 2Tim 4:3
[2] Acts 17:11
[3] Eph 4:15
[4] 1Cor 13:6

disseminating confusion? I would rather have two preachers disagree on the same platform and affirm one another than have them speak contrary words and pretend to agree! The former attitude encourages one to seek and love the truth, whereas the latter produces a disdain for it.

The Bible has so much to say about the truth. We are told to speak the truth, walk in the truth, obey the truth, love the truth and that the truth will set us free. We are also told that, if we do not love the truth, God will send a deluding influence upon us.[5] Is that what has happened? Has God sent us a deluding influence? It does seem that preachers are willing to preach anything today so long as it is deemed "positive." However, should anyone bring a hint of challenge or a morsel of correction it will be labeled "divisive" or a "religious spirit." This is of course a more sanctified type of name-calling.

At this point someone will surely exclaim, "The truth is a person and His Name is Jesus!" Of course! But why do you respond with that? Is it because you seek to honor Christ or because you wish to make truth subjective and based on your personal experience? However, the truth of God's Word is objective and the word of Christ is infallible and not subject to a private interpretation. Thus, all teaching must be based on and in harmony with it.

"All Scripture is inspired by God and profitable for teaching, for reproof, for correction, for training in righteousness; so that the man of God may be adequate, equipped for every good work." 2 Tim 3:16-17

The "All Scripture" in the above verse means that every word in the Bible from start to finish is in harmony and agreement and contains in it all that is needed to establish or correct any teaching that is presented today. Paul the apostle, who gave us those

[5] 2Thess 2"10-12

words, also told us to examine everything carefully and hold on to what is good.[6] Therefore, there must be a place for challenging false teaching and throwing it away without throwing the truth away as well. Yet, these days the mere mention of error will land you a seat with the infamous "Heresy Hunters." These are the multitude of "internet people" who have devoted their lives to what they call "apologetics." Though some of what they say has merit, the problem lies more with the way they say it. Another issue is that the majority, besides lacking grace in their speech, have what seems to be a very narrow view of Christianity with almost no role for the Holy Spirit other than giving us intellectual knowledge. As a result, they declare nearly everyone a "Heretic." Indeed, if you are Charismatic or Pentecostal you are guaranteed to be on the list. This has caused most Christian leaders to despise any kind of corrective teaching whatsoever which is also throwing the baby out with the bathwater. Consequently, almost nothing is examined anymore and all "revelations" are considered valid, unless of course the individual is famous - then they are essential. However, this kind of absurdity places the Apostles of Our Lord on the "divisive" list since they were consistently challenging false teaching and were the first to use the "H" word.[7] Indeed, much of the New Testament is in fact correction of false teachings and teachers.

The word heresy means a belief or opinion that is at variance with the established beliefs and customs. Today however, it is generally viewed as a teaching that is contrary to the core beliefs of our faith and makes the one who originates it an apostate. Yet, the word heresy does not necessarily mean apostasy. This is probably why Peter added the word "destructive" in 2Peter 2:1. Technically, heresy refers to a teaching that is contrary to Biblical teaching and is thus false teaching. It does not necessarily imply that the person teaching it has fallen from the faith or is no longer

---

[6] 1Thess 5:21

[7] 2Pet 2:1

a genuine brother or sister – depending of course on the content of the teaching. This is the problem with labeling someone a "heretic." It implies that they themselves have fallen from the faith and are denying the master - that they themselves are corrupt. However, false teaching is still false regardless of what we call it and all teachers and preachers need to be willing to have their teaching examined for Biblical orthodoxy. A good challenge sends a humble spirit back to the Word to see if the conclusion is correct, whereas, an unteachable spirit will dig in its heels even if they are planted in error. In addition, the number of adherents or movements associated with a teaching or practice does not in itself validate it. Just a casual glimpse at church history will confirm this. Therefore, it is imperative for the sake of the body of Christ that we examine this new teaching on grace that is sweeping the church and do so without attacking the character of those who proclaim it. However, may we also put aside attacks on the character of those who challenge our teaching, and for the good of all, concern ourselves with the accuracy and trustworthiness of the things we boldly proclaim.

Chapter One

The "Grace Revolution"

Have you heard of the "Grace Revolution?" "What is it?" you ask. Is it like the Arab Spring? Well, not exactly. Yet, according to some of its leaders, it will have as profound an effect on the Body of Christ as those recent uprisings have had on the Middle East. It is not a "gentle reformation," they insist, but a "true revolution." A separation between what they call "grace teaching" and "law teaching." A revolt against the "religious legalism and hypocrisy of those who mix law and grace," thereby binding believers in condemnation and bondage, or so they say. According to some, it is sweeping the globe as churches and preachers are joining the ranks daily. Nevertheless, what is it really about and why would it be bad? Is not grace the divine favor of God - the empowering of the Holy Spirit to do what we cannot do and be what we cannot be on our own? We are justified by grace, sanctified through grace, and glorified by His grace. Indeed, "Of his fullness we have all received and grace upon grace" (John 1:16). What then can be wrong with a revolution of grace? Is it any wonder that the ranks are swelling? Who could possibly find fault with it? Is not the gospel of Christ itself the gospel of grace? Did not Jesus come to bring us into grace and Paul say that those who receive the abundance of grace will reign in life? What then is wrong with the revolution and why are pastors and leaders speaking out against it? The answer is actually quite simple. It is contained in the following Scripture:

"For (or because) *the Law was given through Moses; grace and truth were realized through Jesus Christ." John 1:16 Emphasis mine*

The above text says Jesus did not appear bringing grace only and neither does it say there was no grace before He came. What it clearly says is that for or because (Gr. OTI) the Law came through Moses, grace and truth were realized (or came) though Jesus Christ. It does not say that Moses brought the Law but Jesus brought the grace, as is the standard reading. There is no but in the sentence. The Law given by Moses is not being contrasted with or against the grace of Christ but shown to be the preparation for the grace of Christ. Nonetheless, Christ did not bring grace only but He also brought truth. The truth brought by Christ is as essential to us as the grace brought by Christ. We cannot have one without the other. Grace without truth is not really God's grace but something entirely different. Therefore, the problem with the "Grace Revolution" does not actually have to do with grace but the "truth" that accompanies it. To have a true grace revolution we must have a truth revolution as well. Thus, we must take a closer look at the message of this movement and compare it to the truth brought to us by Jesus.

A Brief Summary of "Hyper Grace"

Before we begin, let us understand that this "Grace Revolution," also known as "Hyper Grace," does not claim to have a new release of grace from heaven, or a fresh outpouring of the Holy Spirit. Rather, it claims a new or "restored gospel" that has been purged of commandments and requirements, which it believes will revolutionize the church. According to this message, the Law given by God is the enemy of grace, and if the believer is truly walking in grace there can be no mention of commandments or requirements. The Christian is free from the Law since he died with Christ and has become a new creation. He is now exclusively under grace where there is no law or requirement. He is, in fact, the very righteousness of God and is no longer to receive any condemnation or even conviction, which they perceive to be the same thing. Thus, there is no need for him to repent ever again, since Christ has taken away all of his sins, past, present and future and has not even a record of them. All the believer needs now is education. He just needs to know who he is and get his thinking changed and he has arrived. This is the essence of the "Hyper Grace" message, although there is much more to it as we shall see later.

Fly in the Ointment

As we examine this relatively new message, we immediately see that there is much about it that is true - at least fifty per cent. That of course is the problem. If it did not have a good chunk of truth, most people would not fall for it. It is also why it is so dangerous-because so much of it is true, and even refreshing, that it snares the untaught and unsuspecting. However, the mixture is lethal, yet it is not the grace in the mixture but the error combined with it that will lead to ruin. The all too common plot in detective mysteries reminds us that if you want to poison someone, you must hide the poison in something the victim is eager to consume – where he would least expect it to be. What better than something sweet, something that he cannot resist. Thus, the best place for the enemy to hide his lies at the present is in the grace message we are all consuming. It is the proverbial fly in the ointment – the Achilles heel of the Revival Movement. It is the place where the church is weakest, since, it has distorted the Biblical understanding of Law and Grace from its early days. Consequently, when pastors and teachers confront it they often sound like they are backpedaling because their own understanding of Law and Grace is skewed. Thus, they are easily portrayed as the defenders of tradition and the Law - the "legalists" who have kept us in bondage all these years. In addition, when the message of grace is cloaked in a promise of freedom from "religion" and rules, this young "postmodern" generation of Biblically-challenged, six-month ministry school "equipped" revolutionaries, find it irresistible. Nevertheless, God has a plan in all this. He is flushing something out - bringing it to a head in these last days. In the following chapters, we will not only seek to uncover what is wrong with the "Grace Revolution" but we will also explain what is right and even enlightening about it. We will then go deeper and show how God is exposing the true culprit behind this doctrine and the distortions of Paul's teachings on Law and Grace that have been with us for centuries.

Chapter Two

The Newest New Covenant

Recently I read a quote from a conference speaker, which went something like this: "For us Christians the Ten Commandments are like Ten Promises." Upon reading this, I was absolutely stunned and mystified, not only as to how a preacher could have said such a thing, but that his hearers thought it was good. How in the world do you get promises out of commandments? How does "Thou shalt not steal" become "Thou will not steal?" or "Thou shalt not commit adultery" become "Thou won't be able to commit adultery?" Since when does the "New Commandment" to love one another become a new promise to love one another? When I shared this with the folks in my Bible Class, they were equally stunned and incredulous. "What" they exclaimed! "Are you serious?" Unfortunately, he was serious. However, how does one explain the "logic" behind the Ten Commandments being Ten Promises? I can only presume the point has something to do with being led by the Spirit and thus fulfilling the righteous requirement of the Law (Rom 8:4) and not carrying out the desires of the flesh (Gal 5:16). However, in order to make this point, why would it be necessary to change the commandments to promises since the result is the same? There can only be one answer. Commandments are laws that imply obedience on our part, whereas promises are all about God's loving-kindness and grace.

The Enemy of Grace

"Hyper Grace" preachers believe that the Law is the enemy of grace and they are certainly not alone in this view. The church has been confused about this issue for a very long time. Paul's teaching in Romans and Galatians has been consistently used to say that before Christ came there was no grace and no faith and everyone was just living by the Law which they could not keep. Thus, the whole thing was futile and God instituted the Law just to show us how hopeless we are. Then He intervened and sent Jesus and now we are "under grace" and the law has been done away with forever and we can all breathe a sigh of relief. At least that is how it appears to the Western mind, which is untrained in First Century Hebraic thought and has been offered a translation of these books that is corrupted by Replacement Theology.[8] I taught this position for years since it was the common view, but was never very comfortable with it. It seemed to me that the Ten Commandments cut into stone by the finger of God, and burned into the soul of the Jewish people and Western civilization represented more than a failed experiment that just brought bondage on people. I would read passages like Psalm 19 and 119 and hear David, the man after God's heart, cry out how he loved the Law, and meditated on it day and night, and how it restored his soul. Then I would read Galatians and hear Paul say that Christ redeemed us from the curse of the Law and I began to say to the Lord, "Which is it? Both of these men loved you deeply yet they seemed to see the Law very differently." Later I would understand that Paul was not speaking of the Law (Torah) itself but the curses found in it, and that throughout his writings, He was confronting the real enemy of grace, which is not the Law but Legalism – the self-righteous distortion of Judaism that Jesus Himself confronted. (I have devoted an entire chapter to this distinction later on and will address the common myths and misconceptions about Romans and Galatians and other passages.) However, as we shall see, whatever has been the tension and wrong teaching in the church between the understanding of the New Covenant and the Old, "Hyper Grace" has flown the coup. They have taken Moses to the woodshed, arrested the Ten Commandments, and declared a "grace spring" by putting all

---

[8] Replacement Theology is the idea that the church has replaced Israel as the people of God and that all of the good Bible passages concerning Israel are now for the church. I call this "Religious Anti-Semitism" since it is the origins of Western Anti-Semitism, and is alive and well in the church today.

other "legalists" on notice. They are young, they are zealous, in many cases well-meaning and wanting to right wrongs, but they are devoid of wisdom and experience. They were "fathered" by a generation of celebrity pastors who threw out theology and doctrine and real mentoring for quick success and now they have decided to "divide"[9] the word for themselves. Nevertheless, as Paul said, God is allowing these factions so that those who are approved by Him may become evident.[10] He is forcing the issue. He will insist that we get it right this time. Time is short and if the Bride is to walk in the fullness of God and true unity at the end of the age, she must also come to unity in The Faith.

The Old Covenant Sermon on the Mount

One "Hyper Grace" teacher says it "devastates him" that we teach the Ten Commandments to our children in Sunday school. He finds this so offensive since we are set free from the Law and "our lives in grace will look better than any person trying to keep the Law." In the same article, he says that "the Law is for the unbeliever" and "the only thing a believer needs, to live a holy life, is to remain conscious of the fact that God has fully accepted him as His son, making him a new creation, one with Him and filled with the Holy Spirit, forever."[11] Evidently, he has never taught Sunday school or he believes in infant baptism or something. Tell that to little Johnny the next time he breaks his iPod on his sister's nose or refuses to listen to his teacher. To those of you unaccustomed to this new "grace" message, this may seem like an extreme example of their attitude toward the Law. However, after reading much from a variety of their teachers I find it to be quite consistent. They say they agree with Paul that "the Law is holy and righteous and good"[12] yet it is hard to imagine how they can since they spew out such vitriol against it.

---

[9] "Hyper Grace" teachers consider dividing the word as separating out the passages that speak to our "Pre-Renewed Self" and our "Post Renewed self."

[10] 1Cor 11:19

[11] http://www.phildrysdale.com/2012/10/whats-the-role-of-the-law-in-the-new-covenant/

[12] Rom 7:12

They insist that the New Covenant given by Jesus has no law in it whatsoever and they go to great lengths to establish this, even taking out portions of Scripture and reapplying them to unbelievers or those under the Old Covenant.

Now before I go any further and you misunderstand where I am coming from, I want to make it clear what I believe. I am saved by grace through faith and that salvation is a gift from God. I stand in grace and walk in grace by faith. I am not under law but under grace. No one can be justified by works of any kind. I am filled with the Holy Spirit and live in righteousness as He leads me and I follow Him. I am committed to His wonderful presence in my life and experience it daily. I detest legalism of any kind and consider it an enemy of God. I have also come to understand that God hates striving,[13] and for the last twenty years I have been learning to cease striving and receive the abundance of grace. However, to suggest that by walking in grace I am no longer obliged to obey the Ten Commandments or the commandments of Jesus or confess my sins is absurd. Those who love Him (that has to be believers) keep His commandments[14] and those who keep His commandments abide in His love.[15] Nevertheless, the "Hyper Grace" preachers[16] have found a way around Jesus' words, or so they think. It goes something like this:

"Jesus was under the Old Covenant Dispensation when He said these things. The New Covenant did not begin until after the cross."[17]

With this statement, the HG preachers throw out all of Jesus' teachings as not applying to the church. They do this, of course, to get around all the obvious commandments He gave us. Imagine-the Sermon on the Mount and all of its admonitions were

[13] Ps 46:10
[14] John 14:15
[15] John 15:10
[16] From here on referred to as HG preachers
[17] http://gracerevolution.tv/archives/tag/new-covenant

just for that generation of rebellious Jews and not for believers today, who need only to be reminded of who they are? And of course, the way Jesus taught them to pray, "Forgive us our debts" was Old Covenant, since God has no record of our sins. "How can anyone believe this?" you may ask. Surely, the idea that Jesus came, taught His Disciples for three and a half years, and then made the things He taught obsolete, is absurd? Furthermore, what about the commandments Jesus gave after the cross commanding us to make disciples and teach them to observe all that He commanded?[18]

The HG preachers deny they are dismissing Jesus' teaching along with the Old Testament. It's all Scripture, they say, and important to read, but we must remember to apply it to the right people and not to ourselves since we are in the New Covenant. Thus, they read the Bible and take out what they believe applies to us today, which apparently is very little, and respectfully leave the rest to a time when things were more primitive. This practice undermines all of Scripture and gives them license to reinterpret anything that seems to contradict their message, which of course they do. However, is this really the Biblical New Covenant or a newer version made up by those who hate anything that tells them what to do even if spoken by Jesus Himself? "We don't need commandments and rules," they say. "That's legalism." "We only need to trust Christ in us, and let the Holy Spirit do what He does best." Well of course that is true, but how do we know what "Christ" is in us and what "Spirit" we are following, unless His words are also guiding us? Jesus said that those who heard His words and acted upon them would be like a wise man who built his house upon a rock. He not only spoke this about the Sermon on the Mount but all of His words. He also said that if we were to abide in Him, His words would abide in us.[19] How then can anyone claim to abide in Him and say that the words He was

---

[18] Mt 28:19-20
[19] John 15:7

referring to do not apply to them? Furthermore, did not the Holy Spirit write the entire Bible? Indeed, their favorite apostle, Paul, said that, "All Scripture is inspired by God and profitable for teaching, for reproof, for correction, for training in righteousness…" and this he said about the Old Testament. He did not say God inspired it for another dispensation. On the contrary, he said it was for us and that its teaching, reproof and correction is what trains us in righteousness. Nevertheless, the "Grace Revolution" apparently does not need the training of Scripture or the reproof and correction. One of their teachers said this:

"You see the biggest hindrance to us doing good is our knowledge of good and evil! If we were willing to put aside our desire to do good and avoid evil, and instead just follow God's voice, we would see the most incredible changes in our lives."[20]

Can you believe it? He wants us to put aside our "desire to do good and avoid evil?" How can you do that and have the Holy Spirit? How can you do that and be instructed and trained by the Scripture? This is not only a rejection of the clear teaching of God's Word, but it is a rejection of Scripture itself and woefully ignorant and dangerous. The voice of God will never contradict the Word of God and if it does, it is not God's voice. Of course, they will say that one's interpretation or understanding of Scripture can be problematic and hinder God's voice. Certainly that is true, but isn't that even more reason to approach God's Word with integrity and a humble heart? However, to say that we follow God's voice without the restraint of Scripture (just blind trust in what we hear inside) is to suggest that we are in total harmony with God and there is only purity and goodness inside of us. This of course is what they believe since they are the "righteousness of God," have no more sin in them, and no longer need conviction. They also claim to be in the same equal union

[20] http://www.phildrysdale.com/2012/10/whats-the-role-of-the-law-in-the-new-covenant/

with God as the Father and the Son.[21] More on this later, but for now let us consider what the Bible really says about the New Covenant and its relationship to the Law.

The Real New Covenant

The first mention of the New Covenant in Scripture is Jeremiah chapter 31. It is mentioned again in Ezekiel 36 and quoted in the following passage in Hebrews 8:

"The days are coming, declares the Lord, when I will make a new covenant with the people of Israel and with the people of Judah. It will not be like the covenant I made with their ancestors when I took them by the hand to lead them out of Egypt, because they did not remain faithful to my covenant, and I turned away from them, declares the Lord. This is the covenant I will establish with the people of Israel after that time, declares the Lord. I will put my laws in their minds and write them on their hearts. I will be their God, and they will be my people. No longer will they teach their neighbor, or say to one another, 'Know the Lord,' because they will all know me, from the least of them to the greatest. For I will forgive their wickedness and will remember their sins no more."Heb 8:8-12

Without getting into the issue of the future redemption of Israel and the New Covenant[22] promised them in the Messiah, those of us who belong to Christ both Jew and Gentile, have already entered into that Covenant. (In the future, the Remnant Nation of Israel will enter it as well.) Nevertheless, the Lord says that this New Covenant would not be like the marriage covenant He made with Israel,[23] when He took them out of Egypt, which was all one sided. The people disobeyed the Lord and their hearts were continually straying from Him. This time God promised to make an inner change in the people, taking away their stony hearts and giving them a heart of flesh,[24] where they would all know Him

---

[21] http://www.graceorlando.com/grace-is-neither-hyper-nor-dangerous/
[22] KAINOS could also be translated renewed, but the text suggests both are true
[23] Jer 31:32 "...although I was a husband to them..."
[24] Ez 36:27-28

and be responsive to Him and His statutes. In addition, in this New Covenant, God promised to forgive their iniquity and remember their sins no more. The HG teachers like to focus on this part as proof, that when or "if" we sin, God has no recollection of it and does not even want us to bring it up by confessing it. Nevertheless, God is not saying that His memory is faulty in the New Covenant, but that because of the Blood of Christ, He is faithful to forgive us our sins and cleanse us from all unrighteousness. In other words, for the one who walks in this covenant, sins are cleansed and there is no condemnation. However, it is clearly implied and expected that we are to walk in the covenant and not stray from it. This is the whole point of Jeremiah 31 and the Book of Hebrews, which argues that one can have this great, superior covenant and "drift away from it."[25] Chapter 6, for example, talks about what will happen to those who have been "enlightened," "have tasted of the heavenly gift," and are "partakers of the Holy Spirit" and then fall away from the covenant. Furthermore, how can the HG teachers say there is no law in the New Covenant when the Lord clearly promised to take His Law (Hebrew-Torah, Greek-Nomos) and write it on our hearts by the Holy Spirit?

This glaring omission regarding the Law or Torah of God being written on the heart of the New Covenant believer is not unique to the Hyper Grace movement. Indeed, the church has been either ignorant or intentionally blind to this truth for ages. Yet, the Scripture is clear that the very thing that makes the New Covenant <u>new</u> is the fact that God's Law, or Torah, is written on the heart and no longer merely on tablets of stone. This is the whole point! We are quick to point out that the love of God is poured into our hearts by the Holy Spirit, but what about the writing of God's Law on our hearts? There is not much preaching on that. This is the ministry of the Spirit also. In addition, in all three passages, God says "<u>My Law</u>" – I will put My Laws into their

[25] Heb 2:1

minds and write them on their hearts. When does that happen and how does the Holy Spirit do it? Is the Law that He writes different from what appears in Torah? Does He write just a message of grace and love and peace and no commandments or statutes of any kind? Does He write anything that suggests what is good and what is evil and must be avoided, or is it only nice thoughts about how wonderful we are now that He has finished the work? How can the church claim to be filled with the Spirit and yet hate God's Law - the same Law that the Holy Spirit writes on our hearts? What is the real problem here? How can those who claim to be the righteousness of God hate the righteous requirements of God? Is that not a contradiction? They will say, "The Law is for unbelievers and sinners" to show them the way. Of course, but if one is a new creation and righteous throughout, why would he hate the Law and speak against that which is holy, righteous and good? Could it be that they really don't understand what they are saying and in their zeal are confusing self-righteousness (legalism) with God's Holy Word?

The HG preachers insist that there is no Law whatsoever in the New Covenant. If we bring up any laws, requirements, or commandments that if disobeyed could bring judgment on the believer, they claim we are in an Old Testament mindset. When you point out that there are aspects of Torah that are done away with for the Christian, such as the ceremonial law, the civil law, the sacrificial system, and the kosher laws, but the moral laws still apply, they will cry foul. There is no law whatsoever relevant to the believer. One of their teachers said this:

"You see a lot of people try to break up the law, into either two, ceremonial and moral, or three parts, ceremonial, civil and moral. I often hear people explain that it was the ceremonial law that was nailed to the cross. This is a nice idea we use to try keep a hold of as much of the law as we possibly can, while doing away with some. The problem is the Bible doesn't break up the law as nice and neat as that, in fact it doesn't break

up the law at all. However, I'm not going to argue about whether or not the law is broken up into sections, let's just go straight for the jugular. Paul explains that the "law" which is no longer relevant in the believer's life is ***the law which is "written and engraved on stones"*** *in 2 Corinthians 3:7. Which law does that sound like? The ceremonial law? The civil law? Obviously this is the Ten Commandments Paul is talking about, they were the only laws to be engraved in stone."*[26]*(Emphasis Mine)*

It is peculiar how this preacher complains when we separate out the ceremonial and civil law from the moral laws of Torah, yet He parcels up not only the Old Testament, saying it is no longer relevant, but also the New Testament and even the words of Jesus. However, he is not alone in his twisting of this passage; most modern preachers do the same. Having an attitude toward the Old Covenant as the "ministry of death," they completely distort Paul's words. Incidentally, the same preachers say that God is not a minister of death, and contrary to Scripture, insist that He never put anything bad on anyone.[27] Regardless, Paul is not saying in this passage that God gave the Law to minister death to people,[28] but that the Law brought death as is translated in the NIV. He is not contrasting the Old Covenant and the New, by suggesting one was bad, and the other good. On the contrary, he is saying that both were good and came with great glory, only that the Law, which was written on stone and was not able to change the hearts of the people, resulted in condemnation and death. Thus, he says that he is a minister of the New Covenant Gospel, which comes with much more glory since through the Spirit it changes the heart and causes God's Law to be written on the heart, thereby producing righteousness. The ministry of "the letter" is legalism, which attempts to apply the words of the Law outwardly relying on human effort rather than inward change. This, of course, was the practice of those who opposed Paul's

---

[26]http://www.phildrysdale.com/2012/10/whats-the-role-of-the-law-in-the-new-covenant/

[27] Deut 7:15, Deut 28:61, Acts 5:5, 1 Cor 11:29-30

[28] See Romans 7: 13

ministry, the Judaizers and legalists who took pride in their Torah-keeping. In any event, nowhere in this passage does Paul suggest that the Ten Commandments, which were the letters written on stone, were irrelevant. On the contrary, he concludes the problem was that they were written on "tablets of stone rather than on tablets of the human heart."[29]

In the rest of this passage in 2 Corinthians 3 and 4, Paul goes on to speak of the veil Moses put over his face because the Jews could not look at the glory and how he would take it off when he went before the Lord. Then he says that the same veil lies over the hearts of the Jews who read Moses because they have not turned to the Lord the Messiah. In other words, Paul who knew Christ was able to read Moses and understand and receive while those with the veil could not. Notice, it is not their reading of the "irrelevant Law" which Paul also read, that was the cause of the veil but the condition of their hearts. Then Paul speaks of the glorious freedom we have to approach the Lord, the Holy Spirit, with unveiled face, and to see the light of the gospel of the glory of Christ as in a mirror, and be transformed into the same image from glory to glory. Thus, we cannot separate the gospel of Christ from the glory of Christ nor the commandments of Christ from His transforming power.

Conclusion

Though the love of God is unconditional, the New Covenant is not since it requires the voluntary participation of both parties. God is faithful to all His promises but we in turn must be faithful to Him. The Scriptures are clear on this point.

"Now Moses was faithful in all His house as a servant, for a testimony of those things which were to be spoken later; but Christ was faithful as a Son over His house - whose house we are, ***if we hold fast*** *our confidence and the boast of our hope firm until the end." Heb 3:5-6 (Emphasis Mine)*

[29] 2 Cor 3:3

"For we have become partakers of Christ, ***if we hold fast*** *the beginning of our assurance firm until the end..." Heb 3:14 (Emphasis Mine)*

*"...****if*** *indeed you continue in the faith firmly established and steadfast, and not moved away from the hope of the gospel that you have heard, which was proclaimed in all creation under heaven, and of which I, Paul, was made a minister." Col 1:23 (Emphasis Mine)*

The HG teachers say it is a finished work. We are already perfected and purified and only have to keep being reminded of it. However, this is false. Jesus has perfected His work as the mediator of this covenant, but we are still required to appropriate and walk in its provisions. This covenant is not a slot machine where you have to put in works to receive from God, but neither is it a giant tub of goodies free for the taking. Though righteousness is not achieved through the keeping of rules but by receiving His grace through faith, neither is the heart that does not have the Ten Commandments inscribed on it a New Covenant heart.

Chapter Three

There is Now No Conviction

"Therefore, there is now no condemnation for those who are in Christ Jesus, because through Christ Jesus the law of the Spirit who gives life has set you free from the law of sin and death. For what the law was powerless to do because it was weakened by the flesh, God did by sending his own Son in the likeness of sinful flesh to be a sin offering. And so he condemned sin in the flesh, in order that the righteous requirement of the law might be fully met in us, who do not live according to the flesh but according to the Spirit. Those who live according to the flesh have their minds set on what the flesh desires; but those who live in accordance with the Spirit have their minds set on what the Spirit desires. The mind governed by the flesh is death, but the mind governed by the Spirit is life and peace. The mind governed by the flesh is hostile to God; it does not submit to God's law, nor can it do so. Those who are in the realm of the flesh cannot please God." Rom 8:1-8 NIV

The above verse tells us that there is no condemnation for those who are in Christ Jesus and it also tells us why. The law of the Spirit of Life in Christ Jesus has set us free from the law of sin and death. This law of sin and death is not God's Law as many Bible teachers imply, rather it is the law of sin in our members.[30] It is the old sinful nature we were born with. A greater and more powerful force, that is, the New Nature, the Spirit of Christ or the law (Nomos) of the Spirit, has overcome this law of sin, which is, like the law of gravity that pulls us down. The Law of Moses was unable to do that since it was depending on the flesh and was consequently weak. However, by becoming the perfect sin offering, Christ condemned sin in the flesh in order that the "righteous requirement" of the Law of God might be fully

---

[30] Rom 7:23

met in us who walk according to the Spirit. Notice it is "in order that" or "so that" the righteous requirement "may be" fully met or fulfilled in us. This is obviously the moral Torah or the Ten Commandments. Thus, the believer is not called to judge the Law, attack the Law, and hate the Law but to walk out that portion that still applies to us by the power of the Spirit. Then we are told that the mind set on the flesh is death but the mind set on the Spirit is life and peace; and that the mind set on the flesh is hostile toward God and cannot subject itself to the Law. Incidentally, Paul says that the mind set on the flesh cannot subject itself to the Law, but the grace teachers say it is the mind set on the Spirit that cannot subject itself to the Law. Are you confused? We will discuss this more later. For now, let us consider this whole issue of condemnation and conviction of sin.

No Condemnation

The above passage tells us that there is no condemnation for those who are "in" Christ and then goes on tell us that those who are in Christ walk by the Spirit. Does that mean that once we are born again and receive the Spirit it is automatic? Does it mean that since we are now Christians, and under grace, we are walking by the Spirit and can never experience condemnation or judgment ever again? Apparently, Paul who wrote these words didn't see it that way when he admonished the Galatian Christians to walk by the Spirit and not carry out the desires of the flesh.[31] No doubt, some will say that Paul was not addressing Christians here, but that is absurd, since the letter is clearly written to believers. Besides, in verse 25 he says that "If <u>we</u> live by the Spirit let <u>us</u> also walk by the Spirit." Thus, he emphatically states that one can be made alive by the Spirit or born again, and yet not walk in the Spirit. He goes on to list the deeds of the flesh and the fruit of the Spirit, making it clear that the one who obeys the flesh or practices sin will not inherit the kingdom. That sounds like condemnation to me. However, the "Hyper Grace" teachers flip it

---

[31] Gal 5:16-25

all around. Paul says that the flesh and the Spirit are in opposition and that we cannot do what we please, but they say that it is the Law and the Spirit that are in opposition since the flesh is gone from the scene, having been crucified. However, the Law and the Spirit are not in opposition to each other. It is true that if we walk by the Spirit we are not "under law," or in legalism, but we are not against the Law either. In verse 14, Paul says that the whole Law is fulfilled or walked out by the commandment to love one's neighbor as oneself and that when we walk in the Spirit we satisfy this. Thus, it is not the Law that we are against, but the flesh. Furthermore, it is clear when we put the verses together, as we should, that being "in Christ" means more than simply being a believer. It refers to one who is remaining in Christ[32]walking in the Spirit and continuing in the New Covenant. This does not mean that when or "if" we sin, we lose our salvation or are no longer under grace, but rather it says that if we "practice such things" meaning it is habitual or a lifestyle. With this, the teaching of John concurs when he says that the one who is born of God does not sin, which he defines as "practicing" sin.[33]

The obvious point of this whole passage in Galatians is that Christians should walk in the Spirit and not carry out the desires or cravings of the flesh. Paul lists the deeds of the flesh to make it clear what behavior he is talking about so that no one can say they walk by the Spirit while continuing in those things. The "Hyper Grace" camp responds with verse 24 to say that true Christians who belong to Christ, or are "of Christ," have already crucified the flesh and these admonitions do not apply to them. However, as we have already pointed out, the next verse makes it clear that it is still a choice for the born again (living by the Spirit) believer to crucify the flesh by walking in the Spirit. This is similar to Romans 8:9 where Paul says that if one has the Spirit he belongs to Christ, and then goes on in verses 12 and 13 to say that we who

---

[32] John 15:4 Greek "Meno" means to remain or abide

[33] 1John 3:9

have the Spirit are obliged to "put to death" the deeds of the flesh by being led by the Spirit. Thus, it is not something that happened when we were born again only, or when we were baptized only, but something we must walk in and enforce throughout our lives. This is summed up in Galatians 6 where Paul warns believers that whatever a man sows he will reap, namely; "the one who sows to the flesh will from the flesh reap corruption, but the one who sows to the Spirit will from the Spirit reap eternal life." There is a clear choice for every Christian, to obey the flesh or the Spirit, and the "Hyper Grace" people know it. They found a way to get around the teachings of Jesus, shocking that it is, but what can they do with Paul since he is the "apostle of grace?" One of them has come up with the answer, or so he thinks, and it goes like this:

"Notice that Paul does not say that if a believer sows to the flesh he shall reap "judgment" - just corruption. There is no judgment from God for the sins of a believer. God's judgment for all the sins of the believer, past, present, and future, fell fully upon Jesus. That is the Gospel in its essence. That is the good news!"[34]

Please understand the above is not a typo. He really said that those who sow to the flesh just reap corruption and not judgment. Somehow, in his mind he has found a difference between the two. Paul says that sowing to the flesh is the opposite of sowing to the Spirit; therefore, the fruit has to be opposite as well. However, this pastor insists that corruption is not condemnation and therefore suggests there is no condemnation for the one who sows to the flesh. One can understand why carnal and ignorant Christians would consider this good news. However, this pastor does not want us to think that there is no consequence for sin and sowing to the flesh. Here is his explanation:

"The sins of believers are no longer counted against them because of the death of Jesus. But there is a corrupting power that sin, or the flesh, has

---

[34] http://www.graceorlando.com/grace-is-neither-hyper-nor-dangerous

on the mind of a believer. While the Spirit seeks to renew the mind to unseen realities in Christ thereby releasing the "new creation" in Christ to manifest his righteous identity in word and deed, it is the flesh and the power of sin in the flesh that seeks to corrupt the mind and causes a spiritual "blindness or near-sightedness". While the "new creation in Christ" can be hindered from manifesting his/her identity by means of sinful behavior, inwardly the corrupting power of sin in the flesh is powerless to affect the inward, invisible reality of the "new creation."[35]

For those of you who feel reassured that he admits there is "a corrupting power of sin or the flesh," be careful to read on. This corrupting power only works on the mind but is "powerless to affect the inward, invisible reality of the new creation." Apparently, it can only affect our thoughts and keep us from manifesting our true identity in Christ. Therefore, if I sow to the flesh and find myself committing adultery or fornication or the like, the worst that can happen is that I won't be manifesting the "new creation" that I am? I never have to be concerned anymore about condemnation of any kind regardless of what sin I commit. All that I need, according to these teachers, is to "know" who I am and have my mind renewed. No wonder these churches are packed. The only sin that they seem to consider a real problem and that brings judgment on believers is legalism. However, is this the gospel of Christ "in its essence" or a return to the Gnostic dualism that plagued the early church?

Despite the error of the "Hyper Grace" teaching, we must clearly understand that there is now no condemnation for those who are in Christ Jesus. This is a most wonderful and foundational truth that must be appropriated in order for the believer to walk in the freedom of the Spirit. Far too many Christians are walking around under condemnation because they have failed to either understand or receive what Jesus did for them on the Cross. He absolutely bore all of our sin, past, present and future, and not ours only,

[35] http://www.graceorlando.com/grace-is-neither-hyper-nor-dangerous

but those of the whole world. It is a finished work. Yet, the whole world does not benefit from this reality but only those who have appropriated it by repenting of their sins and trusting in His forgiveness. Indeed, although it is all free, the believer must appropriate everything that Christ accomplished on the Cross. Though we are justified by faith, we must embrace a sanctification process when we come to know Him. We are saved by faith in what Christ has done but we are changed into His image as we continue to walk by faith. Our past sins were cleansed when we repented and accepted the sacrifice of Christ and our present and future sins are cleansed in the same way. Forgiveness was secured by one sacrifice; yet faith, humility, and repentance continue to be necessary for appropriation. The HG teachers say, "It's already done and you just have to catch on and then you will walk it out." "You only sin because you are believing a lie," they say. "Your old man has been crucified and if you are struggling with the flesh it's only because someone told you were." Indeed some of them say we have a "new flesh" since we are a new creation and our new flesh is just immature, makes mistakes, and has to grow up and learn. To them, any thought of having to appropriate it on a daily basis is "coming under the Law." However, this is an utterly false and dangerous teaching, which will lead to shipwreck and ruin. The whole point of Galatians 6:7-8 is to warn the believer about the deception of thinking that he can sow to the flesh and not come under condemnation. In addition, if it were not possible for a born again believer to come under condemnation by sinning, there would be no need for the warning in the first place or most of the New Testament for that matter. Peter warned that God opposes the proud and gives grace to the humble.[36] He was speaking to church leaders, not unbelievers, suggesting that God might oppose them. Furthermore, Paul warned Timothy not to put new believers in leadership lest they become conceited and "fall into the condemnation incurred by the devil." He also warned him not to put younger widows on the list for support

[36] 1Pet 5:5

because they might later on get married and incur condemnation for setting aside their previous pledge. So obviously, a believer can come under condemnation and he can also have it removed by confessing his sins to God and appropriating forgiveness through faith in the finished work of Christ.

Conviction & Conscience

"...having a hope in God, which these men cherish themselves, that there shall certainly be a resurrection of both the righteous and the wicked. In view of this, I also do my best to maintain always a blameless conscience both before God and before men." Acts 24:15-16

The Bible has a lot to say about conscience, especially in the New Testament. The conscience is that inner part of our heart that convicts us of right and wrong. It is the place where we feel conviction of sin or of righteousness. It is a sort of inner buzzer that lets us know what our response should or should not be. But it is more than just a place of conviction. It is also a place of hearing God – a place of knowing with confidence how to believe and act. Thus, it is to be guarded above all. The Proverbs tell us to watch over our heart with all diligence,[37] meaning that we must be careful to examine what we allow in and out. This is an appeal to keep a clear conscience and walk in righteousness. Some will undoubtedly reject this as being "Old Covenant" and claim that we no longer have anything to examine. However, the New Testament Apostles and writers considered the Proverbs applicable to their lives and quoted from them frequently. In the above verse, Paul says that he did his best to always maintain a blameless conscience and he spoke this while walking in the New Covenant. From this simple statement of Scripture, we can draw two conclusions. First, that in Christ it is not only possible to have a blameless conscience, but it is necessary and expected since we believe in the resurrection. Secondly, living with a blameless

[37] Prov 4:23

conscience, where there is no consciousness of sin, requires maintenance on our part. It is not automatic in the New Covenant. It is our responsibility to keep our hearts right with God and as much as possible with man also. Yet the HG teachers say differently. Consider the following:

"I do not deny that sin must be punished, but I am declaring to you that all your sins have already been punished on the body of Jesus. He is your perfect sin offering and we who have received His forgiveness should have no more consciousness of sins. Stop examining yourself and searching your heart for sin. Remember that when someone takes his sin offering to the priest, the priest does not examine him. He examines the sin offering."[38]

"My conviction is that free people will free people. Therefore the greater the freedom we come into the greater the freedom we'll be able to bring others into. The essence of freedom is to know that you are 100% set free from the law and are 100% righteous in Christ - 100% of the time. Bondage is to believe that you are still under the law and not always righteous."[39]

"It's like this illustration: let's say last night you lost your temper while driving and had a bad thought towards and swore in your car towards *the driver. The next morning you wake up, the devil reminded you (because the devil is the accuser of the brethren, God doesn't remind you of your sins it's only the devil) of the event and you felt the condemnation. Then you try to confess yours sins to God out of guilt and self-righteousness, 'Oh God, I'm sorry for the bad temper and swearing in the car yesterday.' Then God says, 'What temper? What are you talking about? I don't remember?' It's as if it never happened, God doesn't keep a record of your sins, He doesn't have any unforgiveness towards you."*[40]

[38] Destined to Reign by Joseph Prince, pg. 187
[39] "No Condemnation Now I Dread!" by Ryan Rufus
[40] http://gracerevolution.tv/archives/category/do-believers-have-to-confess-sins-to-god

The idea that we don't have to examine ourselves anymore and that we are one hundred percent righteous all the time, is the so called "great revelation" of the "Grace Revolution." However, in order to establish it they must annul huge portions of the New Testament by reclassifying them as only applying to unbelievers and make Jesus and the Apostles somewhat bi-polar. Even the warnings of the Risen Savior to the Seven Churches calling for repentance are also relegated to the same category. Presumably, if they had been speaking to these churches they would not have said, "I have this against you," or "I will spit you out of my mouth," or anything like that. On the contrary, it would likely have been, "You guys are awesome, the righteousness of God one hundred percent of the time. Only one thing, there are a few people in your churches who need to get saved and find out how much better they are than they are behaving."

The reason the HG people throw out conviction is that in their minds there is little difference between it and condemnation. Conviction can bring awareness of sin in thought or behavior and this is a problem for them since they maintain all of our sins, past, present, and future are forgiven and cleansed and God has forgotten about them. Thus to bring them up or repent in any way is to disagree with God and walk in unbelief – the one sin they still confront and thus contradict themselves. "The Holy Spirit never convicts us of sin," they say, but "only of our righteousness." Conviction and condemnation are rejected and said to be from the devil. In this way, they also reject conscience and make a grave error since conscience is the God given knowledge that something is either right or wrong.

The Bible has so much to say about the conscience that it is hard to imagine anyone saying we don't have to listen to it. Yet that is precisely what these people are saying who tell us we don't have to examine ourselves or confess our present and future sins. It is the kind of thing you would expect to hear from a Jim Jones or

David Koresh. However, our conscience is such a key component in hearing from God and so important that we are warned to avoid anything that would damage or defile it. Our conscience has to be on board with the things we think and do, and that clearly implies that we can sin by ignoring it. Consider the following verses on the importance of examining the conscience of our hearts:

"I am telling the truth in Christ, I am not lying, ***my conscience testifies with me*** *in the Holy Spirit..." Rom 9:1(Emphasis Mine)*

"Therefore it is necessary to be in subjection, not only because of wrath, but also ***for conscience sake****." Rom 13:5 (Emphasis Mine)*

"But take care that this liberty of yours does not somehow become a stumbling block to the weak. For if someone sees you, who have knowledge, dining in an idol's temple, ***will not his conscience, if he is weak, be strengthened to eat things sacrificed to idols?*** *For through your knowledge he who is weak is ruined, the brother for whose sake Christ died. And so, by sinning against the brethren* ***and wounding their conscience*** *when it is weak, you sin against Christ. Therefore, if food causes my brother to stumble, I will never eat meat again, so that I will not cause my brother to stumble." 1Cor 8:9-13 (Emphasis Mine)*

"Eat anything that is sold in the meat market without asking questions ***for conscience' sake;*** *FOR THE EARTH IS THE LORD'S, AND ALL IT CONTAINS. If one of the unbelievers invites you and you want to go, eat anything that is set before you without asking questions* ***for conscience' sake****. But if anyone says to you, "This is meat sacrificed to idols," do not eat it, for the sake of the one who informed you, and* ***for conscience' sake; I mean not your own conscience, but the other man's; for why is my freedom judged by another's conscience?*** *If I partake with thankfulness, why am I slandered concerning that for which I give thanks?" 1Cor 10-25-30 (Emphasis Mine)*

"For our proud confidence is this: ***the testimony of our conscience,*** *that in holiness and godly sincerity, not in fleshly wisdom but in the grace of God, we have conducted ourselves in the world, and especially toward you." 2Cor 1:12 (Emphasis Mine)*

"....but we have renounced the things hidden because of shame, not walking in craftiness or adulterating the word of God, but by the manifestation of truth commending ourselves ***to every man's conscience*** *in the sight of God." 2Cor 4:2 (Emphasis Mine)*

"But the goal of our instruction is love from a pure heart and ***a good conscience*** *and a sincere faith." 1Tim 1:5 (Emphasis Mine)*

"But the Spirit explicitly says that in later times some will fall away from the faith, paying attention to deceitful spirits and doctrines of demons, ***by means of the hypocrisy of liars seared in their own conscience as with a branding iron****..." 1Tim 4:1-2 (Emphasis Mine)*

"I thank God, whom I serve with ***a clear conscience*** *the way my forefathers did, as I constantly remember you in my prayers night and day..." 1Tim 1:3 (Emphasis Mine)*

"To the pure, all things are pure; but to those who are defiled and unbelieving, nothing is pure, but both their mind ***and their conscience are defiled****." Titus 1:15 (Emphasis Mine)*

"....and ***keep a good conscience*** *so that in the thing in which you are slandered, those who revile your good behavior in Christ will be put to shame." 1Pet 3:16 (Emphasis Mine)*

*"...****keeping faith and a good conscience,*** *which some have rejected and suffered shipwreck in regard to their faith." 1Tim 1:19 (Emphasis Mine)*

The whole idea of keeping a good conscience, one that is clean and sensitive to God, implies regular examination and confession of sin. How else can we keep it clean if there is no confession necessary? Besides, why would we need to maintain a good conscience if there is no consciousness of sins since it would always be pure? Therefore, those who claim that we should not examine ourselves and that we only have to confess our sins when we are first saved, have rejected the need to "keep a good conscience" and have thereby shipwrecked their faith. Surely, it is only a matter of time before the wreckage is found and their recklessness exposed.

In their zeal to deny any warning role for the conscience, the HG teachers appeal to the following passage:

"For the Law, since it has only a shadow of the good things to come and not the very form of things, can never, by the same sacrifices which they offer continually year by year, make perfect those who draw near. Otherwise, would they not have ceased to be offered, because the worshipers, having once been cleansed, ***would no longer have had consciousness of sins?*** *But in those sacrifices there is a reminder of sins year by year." Heb 10:1-3 (Emphasis Mine)*

Under the Old Covenant sacrificial system the sacrifices offered could not make the worshiper's conscience perfectly clean. If they had done so then they would not have to be offered continually, year by year. The worshiper, having been cleansed, would no longer have a consciousness of sins. The passage goes on to say that Christ the High Priest has made the perfect sacrifice, once for all. From this, the HG teachers conclude that Christians should have no further consciousness of sins once they have repented and accepted Christ's sacrifice. Since Christ is the perfect sacrifice, and His blood has washed their sins away, they are not to have any more consciousness of sins, presumably even if and when they sin. In other words, if you lose your temper, and yell at your wife and say mean things to her, you are not to feel any consciousness of sinning. If you do, it is because the devil is using the Law to condemn you. Also, you men who stumble with pornography, when you get offline, there is no reason to repent or feel any consciousness of sin, since it was already taken care of. One HG preacher tells the congregation to repeat after him, "God hates sin consciousness."[41] However, this is a most gross and reckless treatment of one of the most wonderful passages in the Bible and one that will bring real condemnation on the proponents of it. The writer of Hebrews is not talking about how many times a Christian needs to repent. He is not suggesting that the Old Covenant worshiper had to repent continually and we only once. That is ludicrous. He is talking about the inadequacy of the sacrifices to take away sins and the consciousness of them. The sacrifice of Christ, on the other hand, was only needed once to take away all sins for all time. His blood is able to thoroughly cleanse our conscience from evil to serve the living God and it never has to be repeated since it is always sufficient.

"For by one sacrifice he has made perfect forever those who are being made holy." Heb 10:14

When it says that He has made perfect for all time or in perpetuity, it does not mean that the believer is perfectly sinless forever. Rather it is the sacrifice of Christ that was made for all time and will always, in perpetuity, make the one who is "being sanctified" perfectly clean in conscience. Please note the condition. It is for those who are being sanctified or made holy as the NIV says. In other words, the person who belongs to Christ and in the process of ongoing sanctification, is continually, perpetually cleansed and made righteousness by this one sacrifice. For those who are "in Christ" and are "being sanctified" there is forgiveness of sins and no condemnation and no more sacrifices

---

[41]Creflo Dollar, "No More Sin and Condemnation" ttp://www.youtube.com/watch?v=wSCTcLpHiPo

needed.[42] Just as the Old Covenant worshipers came to God, we are exhorted to draw near also, and since we have a perfect sacrifice, we can come into the Holy of Holies, before the Father's Throne.

If we follow the logic of the HG teachers, that the believer never has to do any more confessing or repenting, then why did he need to repent in the first place? Since Christ satisfied the righteous judgment on sin, and God no longer looks at sin or even remembers it, why was it necessary to bring it up at all? Moreover, why would it ever come up again since it has been so thoroughly dealt with? Yet, if we go on reading in Hebrews Chapter 10, it does come up again:

"*For **if we** go on sinning willfully **after** receiving the knowledge of the truth, there **no longer remains** a sacrifice for sins, but a terrifying expectation of judgment and the fury of a fire which will consume the adversaries. Anyone who has set aside the Law of Moses dies without mercy on the testimony of two or three witnesses. How much severer punishment do you think he will deserve who has trampled under foot the Son of God, and has regarded as unclean the blood of the covenant **by which he was sanctified,** and has insulted the Spirit of grace? For we know Him who said, "Vengeance is Mine, I will repay." And again, "The Lord will judge His people." **It is a terrifying thing to fall into the hands of the living God."** Heb 10:26-31(Emphasis Mine)*

It is important to understand that it is only the sacrifice of Christ that cleanses our sin and that the believer has to be engaged in the process of sanctification to receive the perpetual benefit. The HG teachers insist that this passage does not apply to born again believers, and they are not alone in this assertion. Nevertheless, as we have already seen, the whole book was written to Hebrew believers exhorting them not to fall away from the faith. Besides,

---

[42] Heb 10:18

this passage clearly indicates whom it is written to. Consider the following:

"If ***we*** *go on sinning willfully"* – the Writer includes himself.

*"**After** receiving the knowledge of the truth"* – clearly spoken to believers.

"There ***no longer remains*** *a sacrifice for sins"* – these believers once enjoyed the cleansing of Christ' blood.

"…and has regarded as unclean the blood of the covenant ***by which he was sanctified*** – about as clear as it could be that these folks were once sanctified by the blood of Jesus.

Not all HG teachers believe the same things. Some reject the idea that we should not confess our sins and say this is going too far. Yet, their teaching leads people to the same precipice from which they jump. They believe conviction and condemnation are different, but make conviction sound like a cheerleader stripping it of its correcting role. They say things like, "Conviction tells you," "You're too awesome to be acting like that," whereas; "Condemnation tells you you're a rotten sinner." However, this is not the Biblical view of conviction or condemnation and neither is it the way most people experience it. Consider this incident that took place in Antioch:

"But when Cephas came to Antioch, I opposed him to his face, because ***he stood condemned****. For prior to the coming of certain men from James, he used to eat with the Gentiles; but when they came, he began to withdraw and hold himself aloof, fearing the party of the circumcision." Gal 2:11-12 (Emphasis Mine)*

Here Paul says that Peter was guilty and that he stood guilty or self-condemned because he was being hypocritical in his actions.

The implication is that Peter acknowledged his sin, which is the whole point of confession. Nonetheless, the same man who said there was no condemnation for those who are in Christ Jesus was ready to dump a load on Peter because of his fear of the Judaizers. Obviously, he did not believe that a Christian should not feel or be deserving of condemnation. Neither did he believe that this condemnation was coming from Satan, but rather from the Lord because of Peter's actions. Likewise, Peter was surely feeling conviction and obviously condemnation at the same time. It is doubtful he was hearing the Lord saying, "You're too awesome to be acting like this." The text clearly suggests he was feeling some condemnation and shame, which was justified, because of his hypocrisy.

The above example from Scripture illustrates that it is not always easy to distinguish condemnation from conviction, at least as far as the Bible presents it. In addition, there are different levels of both and neither feel good. However, the real reason most Christians can't distinguish between conviction and condemnation is that there really isn't much difference between the two. Both come through the conscience and cause us sorrow and regret and even pain until the situation is remedied. This is the proper working of our conscience and the reason God gave it to us. When we keep a good conscience we stay sensitive to God, and likewise, when we don't, we become hard-hearted and in danger of backsliding altogether. Anyone who denies that they feel their heart hurting when they do wrong, whether intentionally or not, is either lying or possessing a defiled or seared conscience. No one can be tender and responsive toward God, which is what "alive to God" means,[43] and not be sad or sorrowful when they sin and grieve the Holy Spirit. Also, the more sensitive we become to the Holy Spirit, the more we are aware of inner attitudes, thoughts and habits that grieve Him and now us as well. Thus, we learn to co-operate with His leading and navigate away from hurtful

---

[43] Rom 6:11

attitudes, actions and places. This is the process of sanctification and maturing, but it does not mean that we are to go around under condemnation. On the contrary, it is the way that we stay free of condemnation by walking in the Spirit.

We tend to think of conviction as spurring us on to better behavior and condemnation as judgment for our sin and failure. Though there is some truth to this way of thinking, it is hard to substantiate biblically. Romans 8:1 tells us there is no condemnation for those who are in Christ Jesus, but it does not say there is never any condemnation for sin or evil behavior. It goes on to warn us that we must obey the Spirit and put to death the deeds of the flesh.[44] Romans 5 tells us that we are justified by faith and stand in grace and have peace with God, but it is expected that we will continue in this grace through faith and not just receive an introduction.[45] Therefore, it is not that there is no condemnation available for the Christian, but that the Christian no longer needs to live in and receive condemnation since Christ has provided the remedy for it.

What is often overlooked in this discussion is that condemnation can come from several sources. It comes justly upon us as a consequence of sin when we disobey God. However, when we repent of our sins and receive His forgiveness it is no longer justified and we must reject it. Thus, there is legal condemnation and illegal condemnation.

Another source of condemnation, which is the most common among Christians, is self-condemnation. This comes from self-hatred and self-pity or refusal to forgive oneself by receiving God's forgiveness. The conscience of this believer is defiled and he condemns himself even though God has already provided forgiveness. Consequently, this condemnation is also a result of

---

[44] Rom 8:13

[45] Rom 5:1-2

sin – the sin of self-condemnation. Condemnation also comes at us through the judgments of others and the lies of demons. Where there is no basis for this condemnation or judgment, we must reject it standing in the grace and forgiveness of God. However, if there is ground for it and we are opening the door to sin somewhere, it is foolish to reject it since it will not go away. The enemy knows when he has legal ground and will take full advantage of it. Yet, when we repent and close the door and receive God's forgiveness, we can drive him out.[46] Thus, it is foolish to tell believers that they do not have to confess their sins or to examine themselves. Though legalistic and judgmental preachers often overemphasize these things, it is heartless and cruel to take away from believers the very means by which they can appropriate God's grace and healing and live condemnation free.

[46] James 4:7 - Clearly written to believers.

Chapter Four

My Old Man is a Dead Man

The fact that our minds need renewing demonstrates that sanctification is a process and that we must appropriate what Jesus has done. Simply believing that He made provision is not enough. However, appropriating provision is not the same as earning it. Jesus made it available to us but we must receive it. Those who receive (Greek "Lambano" – take hold of) the abundance of grace and the gift of righteousness will reign in life.[47] There is an action involved. We must come before the Throne of Grace to receive grace and mercy in time of need[48]and not merely assume that we have it already. Jesus paid for all our sins so that we could appropriate His forgiveness and healing and not so that we could sin without penalty. He took the punishment for our sins but he has not made us sinless. When we come to Christ and repent, our sins are forgiven and we are washed clean by His blood. We receive a new nature, but we do not receive a "new flesh." If we had a "new flesh", we would have immortal bodies and clearly, we do not. Nevertheless, our old man was crucified with Christ that our body of sin might be done away with or made powerless that we should no longer be slaves to sin.[49]

The old man is the sinful nature that we were born with, which we received from Adam - the inner sin nature that drives us toward rebellion. It's that built-in propensity to sin, which causes a child's first words to be "No" instead of "Yes Mommy." This sinful nature is referred to as the flesh, which operates through and includes the body, but not exclusively. The body itself is

---

[47] Rom 5:17

[48] Heb 4:16

[49] Rom 6:6-7

sometimes referred to as "the flesh" which can be somewhat confusing. In any event, we see this clearly in Romans 6:6 where both appear in the same verse.

"*...knowing this, that our old self was crucified with Him, in order that our body of sin might be done away with, so that we would no longer be slaves to sin; for he who has died is freed from sin." Rom 6:6*

Paul says that the "old man," the sinful nature, or the flesh was crucified with Christ that our physical body would be made powerless. It is powerless because it has lost its power source. The body has a new master, a new nature, the Spirit of Christ. In addition, in his introduction to Romans 7, Paul says:

***"For while we were in the flesh**, the sinful passions, which were aroused by the Law, were at work in the members of our body to bear fruit for death. Rom 7:5 (Emphasis Mine)*

Obviously, Paul had not shed his physical body when he wrote, "While we were in the flesh." What he was saying was that while he was operating in the flesh or the sinful nature, the Law aroused the evil desires in his members. He goes on to detail this struggle between the flesh and the Law in verses 14-24, which many have erroneously dubbed "The Conflict of Two Natures." He was not saying that we Christians should struggle between two natures. On the contrary, he was saying that this was our condition when we were living under the control of the flesh – struggling between the Law and the flesh.

"But now we have been released from the Law, having died to that by which we were bound, so that we serve in newness of the Spirit and not in oldness of the letter." Rom 7:6

When antinomians[50] hear this verse they get excited that the Law has been done away with. In their minds, the Law is the culprit and now that it is gone, we are free. However, though there are aspects of Torah that are replaced by Christ, that is not what Paul is saying at all. On the contrary, he says that we have been released from the Law because we died to that by which we were bound. He did not say that we died to the Law, which bound us but the old nature, the flesh to which we were bound when we were "in the flesh."

When our old man was crucified, it was taken out of the way and the righteous requirements of the Law were satisfied. Now that the Holy Spirit has regenerated our spirits and we have a new nature, we are no longer obliged to obey the flesh but to obey the Spirit. We are no longer enslaved to the flesh but we have become enslaved to the Spirit instead. It is not that the flesh is gone and the Law is gone and there is only a new creation walking around. That day is coming, but it is not here yet. The Law has not gone away but is satisfied with and has no jurisdiction over the one who walks by the Spirit.[51] Should we return to obeying the flesh, the Law will appear with condemnation since we have come back under its jurisdiction.[52] However, when we walk in the Spirit we will not carry out the desire of the flesh and there is no law against the fruit of the Spirit.[53] Thus, we no longer need to comply outwardly with "the letter" which is legalism. Instead, we <u>serve</u>[54] "in the new way of the Spirit and not in the old way of the written code."[55] We are no longer under a system of legalism but under the grace of Christ.

---

[50] Those who are against law – Greek "Nomos"
[51] Rom 7:1
[52] 1 Tim 1:8-11
[53] Gal 5:22-23
[54] Notice we still have to obey or serve God
[55] NIV

Comatose Dead or Rotting Dead

"The sinful nature can't re-vive, so the idea that I have to keep dying to it (e.g. taking up my cross) is untrue; it is not there at all to battle against my Spirit created New self (2Cor5:17). I can't be seduced by a Yin Yang theology of good me versus bad me, any more."[56]

The Bible tells us that our old sinful nature was crucified with Christ. When we enter the baptismal pool by faith, we identify with Christ's death, burial and resurrection and when we come up out of the water, we can now walk in newness of life. However, this does not mean that the "Old Man" was literally crucified on the Cross and is literally laying in the bottom of the pool as the HG teachers insist. Rather, by faith we identify with what Christ has done and apply it to ourselves. We acknowledge that He died in our place on the cross and that our old man was judged, crucified with Him, and buried in the waters of baptism. As we are filled with and renewed by the Holy Spirit we are empowered to walk in newness of life. We do not literally eliminate the old man but we do literally receive a new nature since we receive the Holy Spirit.

When we walk in the Spirit and enforce the victory of Christ by faith, the old nature is overcome and made powerless, but it is not completely gone as the above quote asserts. It is not "rotting flesh that we are still choosing to carry around" but it is in a comatose state because we no longer listen to it, acknowledge it or feed it. However, if the sinful nature did not exist at all, we would not need to be admonished concerning giving it an "opportunity,"[57] "putting to death" its deeds,[58] or not carrying out its "desires."[59] Surely, if the old nature is completely gone, then its evil desires are gone as well and we can no longer have access

---

[56] "Do Christians Still Have a Sinful Nature" by Ryan Rufus
[57] Gal 5:13
[58] Rom 8:13
[59] Gal 5:16

to them. However, it is not gone, as these teachers insist, and we are not "necromancing" by acknowledging this. The Bible is clear that we are to "consider" or "reckon" it dead and ourselves as "dead" or unresponsive to its lusts.[60] We must choose to obey the Spirit and reject the desires of the flesh, which obviously still exist. This is what it means to "lay aside" the old self and "put on" the new self. Paul expressed it this way in Romans 8:

"If Christ is in you, ***though the body is dead because of sin****, yet the spirit is alive because of righteousness. But if the Spirit of Him who raised Jesus from the dead dwells in you, He who raised Christ Jesus from the dead will also give life to your mortal bodies through His Spirit who dwells in you.* ***So then, brethren****, we are under obligation, not to the flesh, to live according to the flesh -for if you are living according to the flesh, you must die; but if by the Spirit you are putting to death the deeds of the body, you will live." Rom 8:10-13 (Emphasis Mine)*

Since Christ is in us, our spirit is made righteous and rejuvenated by His life. Our spirit is alive and responsive to God but our body continues to be dead to God and alive to sin. It remains on the side of sin and sets its desire against the Spirit, which is the reason we cannot follow our desires.[61] The Holy Spirit fills us with His life and gives life even to our bodies so that we have the power to walk in the Spirit and put to death the deeds of the flesh. Paul expressed it this way in Galatians:

"I have been crucified with Christ; and it is no longer I who live, but Christ lives in me; and the life which I now live in the flesh I live by faith in the Son of God, who loved me and gave Himself up for me." Gal 2:20-21

Again, Paul reiterates that the old nature has been crucified with Christ and that Christ lives in us. He then says that the life we

---

[60] Rom 6:11-12
[61] Gal 5:17

now live in the body we live by faith in the Son of God. This is the part the HG message omits – living by faith. By faith, we choose to believe that our old man was crucified with Christ. It is a legal truth that we must apply and walk in. As we trust in the Son of God and allow Him to grow in us, we overcome the flesh with its passions and desires. However, faith is a choice and we still have a choice to obey the Spirit or the flesh. The flesh was not "pulled out by the roots" as they assert, but it is overcome by the believer who walks in the Spirit and gives it no opportunity. This is not to suggest that believers are always struggling with the flesh. On the contrary, as the believer grows in Christ and denies the flesh, the struggle lessens. However, to suggest that there is no struggle at all and that the sinful nature no longer exists is ludicrous. Consider for a moment what the flesh is. Paul gave a list in Galatians 5 to make sure the believers knew what he was talking about and warning them that if they practiced this behavior they would not inherit the kingdom of God.[62] The list includes the following: immorality, impurity, sensuality, idolatry, sorcery, enmities, strife, jealousy, outbursts of anger, disputes, dissensions, factions, envying, drunkenness, carousing and things like these. Please notice that these are not all merely sinful actions that folks engage in but they are a result of yielding to inner passions and lusts and wrong motives and desires. When Paul said, "Things like these" he was implying that this is not an exhaustive list. Other behavior and attitudes, which are addressed elsewhere, such as pride, unforgiveness, stealing, are not mentioned. Nevertheless, the point is that we are to walk in the Spirit and not carry out the desire of the flesh.[63] Obviously then, the flesh still exists and it is possible for a believer to operate in it. However, the HG folks say Paul was not talking to the Galatians about the danger of operating in the flesh but just reminding them that they used to be like this before they got saved, and that there might be a few slackers in their midst who were still unbelievers.

---

[62] Gal 5:21

[63] Gal 5:16

When we consider the list of passions and lusts and evil motives and desires that constitute the flesh, it is shocking to hear HG preachers say that they have no flesh and are one hundred percent righteous all of the time. In other words, they are telling us that they do not sin. Honestly, they never lose their temper with anyone, they never have an impure thought or motive, they never look at anyone with lust in their heart, and they never have envy or jealousy or pride surface in them. They are amazing people and so humble, walking around like Jesus, completely perfect. This is what John meant when he said, "If we say we have no sin, we are deceiving ourselves, and the truth is not in us."[64] In plain English folks, they are lying. However, knowing the foolishness of this stance, some of them admit that they "occasionally" sin.

"Dividing the Word of Truth includes understanding which references are speaking to our position as PRE-Renewed or POST-Renewed. Wrong thinking on the positioning of my POST-Renewed self will give too much power to the appetites of my natural body rather than the power of the Spirit. This will deceive me into thinking I still have a sinful nature to battle....Focusing on the desires of the body can lead to temptation which, uncontrolled, might lead to sin which is evil. (Ja.1:14)....Falling into sin can still happen to the Spirit Renewed self. This sin is not a result of a sinful nature but a mind still renewing."[65]

In the above passage, the author uses Paul's admonition to Timothy to rightly divide or handle accurately the word of truth[66] as an excuse to butcher Scripture into two categories titled "Pre-Renewed Self" and "Post-Renewed Self." He insists that believers no longer have a sinful nature (the flesh) but admits that they can still fall into sin. However, this time it is happening to the "Spirit Renewed Self." How can this be? The New Creation is sinning? Moreover, what causes this Renewed Self, this Brand New

---

[64] 1John 1:8
[65] "Do Christians Still Have a Sinful Nature" by Ryan Rufus
[66] 2Tim 2:15

Creature to sin? Apparently, his unrenewed mind is the culprit. He does not yet understand who he is, but when he does, he will get it right. Therefore, in the meantime he is sinning because someone told him he was a sinner. If he only knew how righteous he was, he would not sin. This is truly remarkable! One would have thought that this New Nature, which is alive to God and "has been created in righteousness and holiness of the truth,"[67]would know the difference between right and wrong and would not have to be taught to do right. How can this be good news? Surely, the "joy" of not having the old sinful man around is overwhelmed by the discovery that the new man is sinful too. Thus in an effort to rid themselves of the old nature by illegal means, the HG teachers tarnish the new nature as well. They deny that the sinful nature exists in the Christian, but blame the mind and the body for the sin that he still commits. However, if the mind and the body are still exhibiting a propensity to sin, then surely they are being influenced by the sinful nature.

We have already seen in Romans 8 that the mind can be set on the flesh or on the Spirit.[68] Therefore, the believer has to set his mind on the Spirit and not the flesh and he must also renew his mind by the Spirit and the word.[69] No doubt, they will argue that when Paul speaks of the mind being set on the flesh, he is talking to unbelievers since he says, "Those who are in the flesh cannot please God." However, the conclusion of the passage is that believers are under obligation to live according to the Spirit and not the flesh, which implies that the flesh is still around and accessible. This is even clearer in the following passage:

"But you did not learn Christ in this way, if indeed you have heard Him and have been taught in Him, just as truth is in Jesus, that, in reference to your former manner of life, you lay aside the old self, which is being

---

[67] Eph 4:24
[68] Rom 8:6-7
[69] Rom 12:1-2

corrupted in accordance with the lusts of deceit, and that you be renewed in the spirit of your mind, and put on the new self, which in the likeness of God has been created in righteousness and holiness of the truth." Eph 4:20-24

This passage clearly identifies itself as speaking to Christians when it says, "you did not learn Christ in this way," and "in reference to your former manner of life." Then the believers are challenged to lay aside the old self, which is identified as the flesh, and to put on the new self and be renewed in the spirit of their mind. Obviously, the flesh has not gone away since they still have a choice to lay it aside.

Are you beginning to understand the foolishness of the HG arguments and the "dividing" and twisting of Scripture that must take place to substantiate them? What desperation brought them to such denial of the existence of the flesh? Yet, they know they cannot dismiss it entirely, because no one can believe that. Instead, this teacher admits there is a danger in focusing too much on "the desires of the body" since that "might" lead to temptation which "uncontrolled might lead to sin." If we give "too much power to the appetites of the body", we might sin. Can you believe it? This pastor believes that the potential for him to sin is minute, and he wants everyone else to believe it as well. However, in spite of his denial of the existence of the flesh, he admits that there "might" be a problem with the appetites of the body if we give it too much attention. At least we agree on that. Yet, if we follow this logic then the only sins a Christian "might" ever fall into are oversleeping, overeating, overdrinking, and immorality. All the other stuff, such as; pride, arrogance, gossip, divisiveness and anger, since they come from inside the soul and spirit of a person, are either no longer sins or they no longer matter.

As stated before, not all HG teachers agree with each other as they try to make the same points. Their level of confusion and twisting of Scripture varies. For instance, this one admits that we still have an old nature, and with a sort of Gnostic rationale, makes it irrelevant to the believer's spiritual condition, even if he yields to it.

"On another level, in the spiritual world, the believer will experience the corrupting power of sin in spiritual matters as a consequence of a lifestyle of sin."

While admitting that there is a corrupting power of sin because of a "lifestyle of sin" he goes on to say that it does not really matter.

"The sins of believers are no longer counted against them because of the death of Jesus. But there is a corrupting power that sin, or the flesh, has on the mind of a believer. While the Spirit seeks to renew the mind to unseen realities in Christ thereby releasing the "new creation" in Christ to manifest his righteous identity in word and deed, it is the flesh and the power of sin in the flesh that seeks to corrupt the mind and causes a spiritual "blindness or near-sightedness". While the "new creation in Christ" can be hindered from manifesting his/her identity by means of sinful behavior, inwardly the corrupting power of sin in the flesh is powerless to affect the inward, invisible reality of the "new creation". [70]

Again, we have the assertion that the mind simply needs renewing or reprogramming for the believer to stop sinning. There is no judgment for the sins that believers commit and no consequences either, since the corrupting power of sin he experiences in "spiritual matters" because of a "lifestyle of sin" is powerless to affect the inward "new creation." Another very well-known teacher insists that since the old flesh is crucified we now have a "new flesh" that just needs to grow up and learn.

---

[70]Grace is Neither Dangerous nor Hyper, Bill Snell - http://www.graceorlando.com/grace-is-neither-hyper-nor-dangerous/

"If you were taught that Christians are supposed to sin, then literally, grace was not released on you to be free from it. This is not condemning you I'm giving you grace – look you don't have to live like that. It isn't that you're not gonna get to heaven if you do, it's like why do you want to live like that? Why do you want to? You don't need to! So you're saying – ok what you're saying is that I shouldn't be struggling. No, I didn't say that. I said you shouldn't be struggling with your old man. It is true- it is true, that your flesh, your new man, needs to grow and learn. Even Jesus – it says that Jesus learned obedience through the things he suffered. How many of you know Jesus never sinned but He still had to grow even though He was a sinless man? How many of you know that your flesh has things to learn? I am not saying that your flesh, your new man, doesn't have things to learn and that he doesn't have to grow and he doesn't have to grow up."

This pastor insists we have a "new flesh" which he claims has replaced the "old flesh" or the "old man" that was left in the baptism pool. He gets this concept of a "new flesh" from Ephesians 5, where Paul in his analogy concerning how husbands ought to love their wives as their own bodies, says, "No one ever hated his own flesh, but nourishes and cherishes it." Thus, he declares, since Paul is telling us to nourish and cherish our bodies we have a "new flesh" because he would not have told us to nourish and cherish the "old man." How ridiculous! Paul was merely saying that since the wife and the husband are one flesh, the husband ought to love his wife as himself, and that nobody has ever hated his own flesh – meaning his own physical body. When he says no one does or ever has, obviously he is not talking about some difference between a believer's body and an unbeliever's body. Moreover, to say that our bodies are now part of something called the "new flesh" is to say that our new nature now incorporates the physical body, which still has corruption in it. In addition, if this were true then the physical body of the believer would no longer want to sin and would be just as sensitive to the Holy Spirit as his spirit man is. Not only is this intellectually absurd, it is a contradiction of many Bible passages.[71] Yet, the church goes wild after these teachings. Our bodies are sanctified through the presence of the Holy Spirit, even though they still have, sin, corruption and death in them. That is why we are warned to obey the Spirit and not the fleshly desires of our bodies.

Sinners or Saints

The renewing of the mind is indeed a big part of walking in sanctification but it is by no means the only responsibility for the believer. We are obliged to keep our hearts right toward God and others and to walk in a manner worthy of the gospel. The Bible exhorts us to be sanctified throughout, spirit, soul and body, and to be found blameless at His coming.[72] As we have said before, this means that we are maintaining a good conscience and submitting to the sanctification process. The HG teachers tell us that we already are sanctified throughout and "if" we sin, it is only because we don't know who we are.

"If you believe you are sinner, then you'll sin by faith. If you believe you are an 'Idiot', then you'll act like a Idiot. The whole bible is all about transforming your mind, there is nothing you have 'To Do', it has already 'Been Done!', just Repent (change your mind) and Believe the Truth so you can be Set Free!!!"[73]

The statement that we have "nothing to do" only to "change our minds" is a contradiction. Paul tells us to not be conformed to this world but to "be transformed" by the renewing of our minds.[74] He puts the responsibility squarely on us, to change our thinking. Through applying the word of God, the believer has the responsibility to change the way he thinks and thus begin to fulfill the will of God for his life. However, there is a whole lot more

---

[71] Rom 8:10 (body is dead because of sin), Rom 6:12 (it's lusts), 1Cor 9:27, 1Pet 2:11, 1John 2:16
[72] 1Thess 3:13,5:23, 2Cor 7:1
[73] http://gracerevolution.tv/archives/category/do-believers-have-to-confess-sins-to-god
[74] Rom 12:1-2

going on when a believer sins than merely wrong thinking. There are often wrong motives, wrong attitudes, judgments, rebellion, lust, pride, anger, unforgiveness, lying and other issues of the heart involved. To say that sin is merely a matter of not knowing who you are is to say it is simply the result of ignorance. In other words, since you don't really know the royalty that you are, you can't stop sinning. But once you are taught by these "enlightened" teachers you won't sin anymore – right? The problem with this teaching of course is that it is false. Furthermore, the believers who receive it are likely to sin more and experience more condemnation than they ever did before. This may seem like a needless charge but unfortunately, it is true. Believers struggling with sin already know they are doing wrong. This is the reason they feel condemnation. Christians that are struggling with pornography, anger, or bitterness, are aware that they are sinning. They likely need ministry to help them appropriate the freedom of Christ and then the faith and discipline to walk in it. Telling them that they are royalty will probably make them feel better temporarily, but it will likely increase the guilt the next time they stumble because they now know they are "too good to be acting this way." Honestly, to hear a famous Christian leader say, "I didn't stop sinning until I finally realized I wasn't a sinner," is nauseating. What do you mean? You don't sin anymore, ever? And all it took to become sinless was the knowledge that saints are not sinners? Is that really true? Do these people stop sinning entirely, or do they simply change their definition of sin and sinning?

The "great revelation" of the HG folks is that saints are no longer sinners. We are not sinners saved by grace but we are saints or holy ones. This is absolutely true and I have known it almost all my Christian life. However, they are twisting it somewhat by saying that saints don't sin at all or don't struggle with sin. Nevertheless, it is not a complex truth or difficult to explain. Sinners are people who practice sin. Sin is what they do. They live a life of sin. When you become a genuine believer, your sins are forgiven and you receive the Holy Spirit. The Holy Spirit's presence in you makes you a saint. You are no longer a sinner because you no longer practice sin. This does not mean that you do not sin at all when you become a Christian. It means that you now practice righteousness and not sin.

In an attempt to explain their version of it, the HG teachers carve up 1John into two sections, one they say is for Gnostics and the other for true Christians. In this way, they get around passages that contradict them and believers who are ignorant of the word fall into the trap. Perhaps the best way to explain how they reach their erroneous conclusions is to go through the passages themselves bearing in mind that all of the concepts mentioned have to be put together to fully understand the meaning. We will begin with 1John 1:5-10:

"This is the message we have heard from Him and announce to you, that God is Light, and in Him there is no darkness at all. Vs. 5

The theme of darkness here is sin. Sin is darkness and there is no sin in God.

"If we say that we have fellowship with Him and yet walk in the darkness, we lie and do not practice the truth" Vs. 6

Please notice the use of the personal pronoun "We" which means "Us" or "I" plus "Them." The HG teachers say that John was speaking these verses to Gnostics, which of course is ridiculous since he wrote it all to his "children," the church, and included himself in every sentence. Surely, John was not a Gnostic. Herein lies the intellectual dishonesty of the HG movement in their obvious butchering of the Epistle to fit their desired meanings.

John says that if **we** (himself included) say we have fellowship with God and **walk** (meaning live in) darkness, we lie and do not **practice** (doing) the truth. Notice the focus is on practicing or walking in the truth as a lifestyle. John reiterates this again in Chapter 2 and this time makes it clear what practicing the truth means.

"The one who says, "I have come to know Him," and does not keep His commandments, is a liar, and the truth is not in him; but whoever keeps His word, in him the love of God has truly been perfected. By this we know that we are in Him: the one who says he abides in Him ought himself to walk in the same manner as He walked." 1John 2:4-6

Knowing him, abiding in Him and having fellowship with Him all have the same meaning, and the one who says he has this fellowship and does not keep His commandments is not walking in truth and is a liar.

"...but if we walk in the Light as He Himself is in the Light, ***we*** *have fellowship with one another, and the blood of Jesus His Son cleanses us from all sin." Vs. 7*

The "but" in the beginning of the sentence shows that it is a deliberate contrast with the previous statement, which says that we cannot have fellowship with God and not walk in truth. However, if we walk or live in the light or the truth, and keep His commandments, we do have real genuine fellowship with God. This is the meaning of "fellowship with one another" – God and us. Then John says that if we have this real fellowship with God that the blood of Jesus His son cleanses us from all sin. Wait a minute- are you getting this? The HG teachers say all our sins, past, present and future, are cleansed the first time we repent and come to Christ and we never have to confess sin again, and that God has forgotten it and we are not to be conscious of it. However, John says that if we are practicing the truth and walking in the light and have genuine fellowship with God, then the blood of Jesus cleanses us from all sin. This suggests that even though we are keeping His commandments, and walking in truth as a lifestyle, and having wonderful fellowship with God, there is still sin that needs to be cleansed. Also, please notice that John includes himself in all this. Thus, despite the fact that we are in fellowship with God and under grace, there is still sin that needs to be confessed and cleansed. Indeed, it is precisely because of our fellowship with God that all remaining sin or sinfulness is cleansed.

If we say that we have no sin, we are deceiving ourselves and the truth is not in us. Vs. 8

This sentence cannot be disconnected from the preceding one. If we (those having fellowship with God) say we have (present tense) no sin (sinless), we are deceiving ourselves and the truth is not in us. The HG teachers know that this verse and the one following sink their ship, so they have to say John was writing to Gnostics or unbelievers who didn't know God. But that is impossible since they are written about those who walk in the truth and have fellowship with God, and John is included. If John had said, "If they say they have no sin they lie and the truth is not in them," then the HG folks might have something to consider here. However, John uses personal pronouns throughout the sentence when he says, "If we say" and "we are deceiving ourselves" and the truth is not "in us." Then he contrasts this deceptive behavior of denying that we have any sin, with the correct response of Christians who walk in the light.

If we confess our sins, He is faithful and righteous to forgive us our sins and to cleanse us from all unrighteousness. Vs. 9

It is impossible to separate this verse from the ones preceding it, without deliberately twisting its meaning. Also, please notice the conditional "if" before each sentence; "if" we walk in the light the blood of Jesus cleanses us, "if" we say we have no sin we are deceived, and "if" we confess our sins He is faithful and righteous to forgive us. All of these conditions are applied to those who walk in the light and not unbelievers. They are deliberately intended to convey the message that one cannot be in fellowship with God without walking in the light and acknowledging sin and confessing it when necessary. The next verse and the following first five verses of chapter two cannot be interpreted separately since they are also part of the same discussion.

If we say that we have not sinned, we make Him a liar and His word is not in us." Vs. 10

John has already stated that we Christians cannot say that we have no sin, or we would be lying. Now he adds that if we say, "we have not sinned" we make God a liar and the truth is not in us. It is true that this verse can be applied to the Gnostics or unbelievers who say they haven't sinned before they come to Christ, but it can equally be applied to believers who say they have not sinned and that they presently have no sin. This whole passage, and most of 1John, is written to make a clear distinction between Gnostics and real Christians. That is the whole point. Consequently, it is very clear that John is outlining how a true Christian differs from a Gnostic. For instance, he says true Christians don't deny that they have sin or that they have sinned. They do not claim to have fellowship with God while they disobey His commandments. Instead, they walk in the light, as God Himself is in the light, confessing their sins, known and unknown, and as a result are washed in the Blood and cleansed from all unrighteousness. The Gnostics, on the other hand, deny that they have sinned or that they have any sin at all. They do not walk in the light acknowledging their sins, and receiving Christ's cleansing, and because of this they are not truly fellowshipping with God and are not real Christians. Thus, the HG folks identify themselves as having the same profession as Gnostics.

"My little children, I am writing these things to you so that you may not sin. And if anyone sins, we have an Advocate with the Father, Jesus Christ the righteous; and He Himself is the propitiation for our sins; and not for ours only, but also for those of the whole world." 1John 2:1-2

Now John wants to make it clear to his "little children" that he is saying these things so that they won't sin. Presumably, he is concerned that they might have gotten the wrong idea from the previous verses. He doesn't want his hearers to think that he is being soft on sin and saying that since they are cleansed by the Blood it is no big deal if they sin. On the contrary, he wants them to walk in the light and have uninterrupted fellowship with the Father. Then he says, "If anyone sins we have an advocate with the Father." The HG teachers use this verse to suggest that sinning should be very rare for a true Christian because John said, "If anyone sins." They take the "if" to mean that it is an exception for the believer and not something that is expected. Though there is truth to this, before I examine it, I want to illustrate how it is being misused by the HG message.

As we have seen, the HG teachers say that all of our sins past, present, and future were washed away when we first came to Christ. God no longer has any consciousness of our sins and neither should we. They dismiss the writings of 1John in the following manner:

"Unbelievers need to confess their sins to God to get saved; but Christians do not need to, because they are already saved. 1John 1:9 was written to refute the teaching that Gnostic false teachers had infiltrated the church to dilute the Gospel Message to the world. The Gnostics claimed that 'there was no such thing as Sin or Sinning' and that our bodies are already evil anyway. So what John the Apostle was essentially saying was,

'If any unbelievers confess their sins, they can be cleansed of all their sins and get saved.' If an unbeliever doesn't believe that 'sin or sinning' exists (or the doctrine of original Sin) due to the Gnostics teaching that was trying to infiltrate the believers, then the unbeliever won't acknowledge that he is a sinner to God and hence be saved."[75]

Though not all HG teachers agree on how they reach their conclusions, the above quote is the standard position on 1John. Notice how the author admits that Gnostic teaching infiltrating the church was the problem but goes on to say John was addressing those outside the church. He says that John is concerned that unbelievers might not believe they are sinners needing to repent and be saved, because of the Gnostic teaching that was infiltrating the believers. In other words, 1John was more concerned about people not being saved because of Gnosticism, rather than Christians being deceived by Gnosticism. This is a diabolical twisting of Scripture and one has to be in complete denial of truth to accept it. However, it is very clear that John wrote his Epistle to the churches warning them to stay faithful to the truth and to renounce Gnostic teaching, which he called "Antichrist." Moreover, the two main Gnostic doctrines he warned Christians to reject are first, the idea that they do not have any sin to confess, and secondly, that the Messiah has not come in the flesh. Thus, the HG teachers who say Christians have no need to confess sin or have any consciousness of sins are declaring their agreement with the Gnostics.

Some who are preaching HG are uncomfortable going as far as to say a believer does not have to confess sin. They acknowledge that 1John 2:1 leaves some wiggle room should a Christian sin but focus on the "if anyone sins" to claim that sinning should be very rare among Christians. Consider the following excerpt from a well-known teacher in an extremely popular movement. I am omitting the reference since he has not, to my knowledge, fully

---

[75] http://gracerevolution.tv/archives/category/do-believers-have-to-confess-sins-to-god

embraced the HG movement even though his teachings are seriously aligned.

"If you say that you don't sin you are a liar. What's he talking about? You can't come to Jesus as a non sinner. You can't say, you know, I'd love to come to you but I didn't sin. He's saying you can't do that. You have sinned. If you say that you haven't sinned you're a liar. But once you receive Christ, what's supposed to happen? You're not supposed to sin anymore."

By this, he acknowledges that he believes that John was addressing Gnostics or non-Christians. Once you become a Christian, he says, you are not supposed to sin anymore.

"Then he goes, wait a second, if you do, you have an attorney. If you do. Not when you do, if you do.....He's leaving a little room, like, alright, alright, alright, alright, you might sin – once in a while and need an attorney. Do you understand that when you sin you need an attorney? Do you know why you need an attorney? Because He took away every excuse you have for sinning. So now you need an attorney to defend you. You need an attorney to defend you because you have no reason to sin. He says, listen, if you sin, Jesus will represent you in court. If you do!"

James says that we all stumble in many ways,[76] but not this preacher. He claims that John was "leaving a little room" just in case we sin. Obviously, his view of sinning or stumbling has to be different from that of James. We will find out later that it is. In any event, he quotes the whole passage where John explains clearly, what he means by the statement, "No one who abides in God sins," but he fails to explain it. Rather it is clear that he ignores or doesn't understand the "practicing" part. Nevertheless, John is speaking about practicing sin. No one who is born of God practices sin or lives a lifestyle of sin. As we have seen before, this does not mean that Christians do not sin. It means that those who

---

[76] James 3:2

truly know God do not practice sin. However, they cannot say they have no sin but as they walk in the light and confess their sins, God is faithful and righteous to forgive them and to cleanse them from all unrighteousness.

This pastor differs from the others, in that they say God has no more memory of sin and we have no need to confess them, while he says we should not have any sin, period. And if anyone should sin, then they need an attorney to represent them in court. Can you imagine? Every time you stumble, you have to go to court. Is that what James meant? Did he have to go to court often? It appears that the Hebrews were in big trouble also, since they were believers and still struggling with sin.[77] This is actually the most condemning thing I have ever heard and this pastor knows it. Yet, he is emphatic that if you are sinning or struggling with sin, you are not born of God.

"You say, 'Oh man, I'm struggling, I'm struggling with sin.' Listen, don't get upset. If you were taught, if you were taught that Christians are supposed to sin, then literally, grace was not released on you to be free from it. This isn't about condemning you, I'm not condemning you, I'm giving you grace. You don't have to live like that. It isn't that you're not going to get to heaven if you do, it's, you know, why do you want to live like that? Why do you want to? You don't need to."

I believe that this pastor means well, and that he doesn't want Christians to sin. But now in an effort to explain himself he transforms the "little wiggle room" into the Grand Canyon. He admits that Christians sin, but declares that it is because they have been taught that "Christians are supposed to sin." Therefore, grace has not been released on them because of the wrong teaching. What? Being born again is not sufficient grace to stop sinning? This contradicts his statement that "those who are born again do not sin" into "those who are born again and have the right

---

[77] Heb 12:1,4

teaching do not sin." He asserts that we don't have to "live like that." I agree! Christians do not have to live in sin or practice a lifestyle of sinning. If they do that, they don't know God. But then he says that if you do "live like that" you are still guaranteed heaven, it's just that you don't have to live like that. Are you a tad confused? I would say that this man is very confused, but sadly the fans are eating it up. Yet, there is more.

"So you're saying, ok, so what you're saying is that I shouldn't be struggling. No, I didn't say that. I said you shouldn't be struggling with *your old man. It is true, it is true, that you're flesh, you're new man, needs to grow and learn." Even Jesus – it says that Jesus learned obedience through the things he suffered. How many of you know Jesus never sinned but He still had to grow even though He was a sinless man? How many of you know that your flesh has things to learn? I am not saying that your flesh, your new man, doesn't have things to learn and that he doesn't have to grow up. Am I saying that you never have a problem with your flesh? No, I'm not. I'm saying that your flesh is immature, it needs to grow up, it learns through the things it suffers just like Jesus learned through the things He suffered. That's a whole lot different than I'm prone to do evil."*

To make matters worse he insists he is not saying we shouldn't struggle. On the contrary, we do struggle but not with the flesh or the old man but with the "new flesh" or new man. Really? How can this be? How can we struggle with the new man? Is our struggle with Christ? Moreover, if we are not struggling with sin, what are we struggling with? His response is that our new man has to grow and makes all kinds of mistakes because he is immature. By this he redefines sin to convince himself that he does not sin or struggle with sin.

"There is a difference between a mistake and a sin. The only way you can sin is to know what you are doing is wrong and do it anyway."

This definition of sin as being only a deliberate act of defiance is not a Biblical view of sin, but it explains why someone would say that he could go a whole day or a whole week without sinning. Actually, if one can go that long without sinning then perhaps a month, six months or a year, or longer would also be achievable. However, if you view sin the way the Bible does then you will see that this is an arrogant attitude that is inconsistent with godliness.

Deliberate defiance of God's commands is serious sinning, but it is not the only way or the most common way that believers sin. We also sin when we don't do things we should or fail to be as kind and gracious as we should. We can sin by entertaining thoughts, motives, and desires that are wrong. We can sin without knowing it and hurt or offend another person's conscience. We can sin by not living in thankfulness. We can grieve the Holy Spirit by things we are not even aware of, such as coarse jesting.[78] Every word we speak that is unkind, careless, or lacking in love is sin. Every thought that we entertain (not just have) that is contrary to God or His word is sin. We can lash out in anger without meaning to. We can hold unforgiveness against a person and not be aware of it until God exposes it. We can sin by shrinking back in our faith and not fulfilling the call of God on our lives. We can sin by causing another person to stumble even though we didn't mean to. The one who claims not to have any sin is completely pure in spirit, soul and body and not only never disobeys God, but does God's perfect will all the time in their lives, perfectly. Is this the goal for us? Yes! However, we will not fully arrive at perfection until we shed this mortal body and put on one that is immortal and pure. Consider these Scriptures that clearly defy the above definition of sin.

"If a person ***sins unintentionally*** *in any of the things which the LORD has commanded not to be done, and commits any of them, if the anointed priest sins so as to bring guilt on the people, then let him offer to the LORD*

[78] Eph 5:4

a bull without defect as a sin offering for the sin he has committed." Lev 4:2-3 (Emphasis Mine)

"Who can discern his errors? Acquit me of hidden faults. Also keep back Your servant from presumptuous sins; *let them not rule over me; then I will be blameless, and I shall be acquitted of great transgression. Let the words of my mouth and the meditation of my heart be acceptable in Your sight, O LORD, my rock and my Redeemer." Psalm 19:12-14 (Emphasis Mine)*

"Pray, then, in this way: 'Our Father who is in heaven, Hallowed be Your name. Your kingdom come. Your will be done, on earth as it is in heaven. Give us this day our daily bread. ***And forgive us our debts****, as we also have forgiven our debtors. And do not lead us into temptation, but deliver us from evil." Mt 6:9-13 (Emphasis Mine)*

Notice, one of the things Jesus told us to do daily is to ask for forgiveness of our trespasses. We know He was meaning daily because he also told us to ask for our daily bread. This does not necessarily mean we have to seek forgiveness for something daily (this can be unbelief), but it shows a heart of humility and one that appropriates His forgiveness and grace every day.

"But he who doubts is condemned if he eats, because his eating is not from faith; and whatever is not from faith is sin." Rom 14:23

"For I am conscious of nothing against myself, yet I am not by this acquitted; but the one who examines me is the Lord." 1Cor 4:4

Notice the humility of Paul's attitude and compare it with that of the HG teachers. Though he is not aware of any sin in His life he says that he is not by this knowledge acquitted, but the one who examines him is the Lord. All Godly people know they have to keep their hearts pure before the Lord, and that there may be something in them that only He sees. They also know it is the

Word of God that exposes the thoughts and intentions of the heart that are displeasing to Him.

"Therefore I run in such a way, as not without aim; I box in such a way, as not beating the air; but I discipline my body and make it my slave, so that, after I have preached to others, I myself will not be disqualified." 1Cor 9:26-27

Obviously, Paul did not believe he had a new flesh that needed to be pampered. Instead, he says he buffets his flesh and subdues it lest its desires ensnare him and he become disqualified.

"Therefore, having these promises, beloved, ***let us cleanse ourselves from all defilement of flesh and spirit****, perfecting holiness in the fear of God." 2Cor 7:1(Emphasis Mine)*

Paul, like John, includes himself in this verse when he says, "let us cleanse ourselves." Cleansing ourselves from all defilement obviously implies repenting, confessing, and applying the blood of Jesus to every part of us. It is clear that he believed there is maintenance involved and an ongoing process of sanctification.

"And this I pray, that your love may abound still more and more in real knowledge and all discernment, so that you may approve the things that are excellent, ***in order to be sincere and blameless until the day of Christ;*** *having been filled with the fruit of righteousness which comes through Jesus Christ, to the glory and praise of God." Phil 1:9-11(Emphasis Mine)*

The clear belief of the Apostles of our Lord was not that it was a one time, finished work we received when we were saved, and we are one hundred percent righteous all the time. They saw a process of walking it out and staying sincere and blameless until His coming.

*"**Not that I have already obtained it or have already become perfect**, but I press on so that I may lay hold of that for which also I was laid hold of by Christ Jesus." Phil 3:12 (Emphasis Mine)*

Many of the HG teachers claim to have reached perfection, since they have no more consciousness of sin. Obviously, Paul did not consider himself perfected.

*"Now may the God of peace Himself **sanctify you entirely**; and may your spirit and soul and body be preserved complete, without blame at the coming of our Lord Jesus Christ. 1Thess 5:23 (Emphasis Mine)*

This is a clear statement of the ongoing process and maintenance of sanctification.

*"It is a trustworthy statement, deserving full acceptance, that Christ Jesus came into the world to save sinners, **among whom I am** foremost of all." 1Tim 1:15 (Emphasis Mine)*

Was Paul getting bad teaching?

"Do *not lay hands upon anyone too hastily and thereby share responsibility for the sins of others; keep yourself free from sin. Tim 5:22*

This is an example of how we can sin unintentionally through lack of wisdom and how Paul insists we must keep ourselves free from sin.

*"But encourage one another day after day, as long as it is still called "Today," so that none of you will **be hardened by the deceitfulness of sin."** Heb 3:13 (Emphasis Mine)*

Not only can Christians sin, they can be deceived and hardened by it.

"For the word of God is living and active and sharper than any two-edged sword, and piercing as far as the division of soul and spirit, of both joints and marrow, ***and able to judge the thoughts and intentions of the heart.*** *And there is no creature hidden from His sight, but all things are open and laid bare to the eyes of Him with whom we have to do." Heb 4:12-13 (Emphasis Mine)*

"...but into the second, only the high priest enters once a year, not without taking blood, which he offers for himself and ***for the sins of the people committed in ignorance.*** *Heb 9:7(Emphasis Mine)*

"Therefore, since we have so great a cloud of witnesses surrounding us, let us also lay aside every encumbrance ***and the sin which so easily entangles us,*** *and let us run with endurance the race that is set before us..." Heb 12:1(Emphasis Mine)*

Again, not only is the author speaking to believers, he includes himself.

"You have not yet resisted to the point of shedding blood ***in your striving against sin..."*** *Heb 12:4 (Emphasis Mine)*

The Hebrew believers are told that they have not resisted so much so as to shed blood in their struggle against sin. However, the HG teachers say there is no struggle for the believer against sin.

"But if you show partiality, you are committing sin and are convicted by the law as transgressors." James 2:9

"Therefore, to one who knows the right thing to do and does not do it, to him it is sin." James 4:17 (Emphasis Mine)

"Therefore, ***confess your sins to one another****, and pray for one another so that you may be healed. The effective prayer of a righteous man can accomplish much." James 5:16 (Emphasis Mine)*

Sin is Sin?

The Bible makes it clear that those of us who are in Christ have been delivered from the power of sin, and that we are no longer to allow it to operate in our lives. Yet, it is also clear that if we say we don't have any sin we are deceived. How do we reconcile these two thoughts? When we study the Epistle of John, these difficulties are presented but are also answered. Indeed, the answer is very simple, when we put the verses together and understand the Apostle's view of sin.

"If anyone sees his brother committing a sin not leading to death, he shall ask and God will for him give life to those who commit sin not leading to death. There is a sin leading to death; I do not say that he should make request for this. All unrighteousness is sin, and there is a sin not leading to death." 1John 5:16-17

The HG teachers, for obvious reasons, do not address this verse. However, it is the answer to the question. John says there are two types of sin, one leading to death and one not leading to death. Paul is very emphatic on this as well in Gal 5:19-21 when he speaks of the deeds of the flesh that if practiced will disqualify the believer from heaven. These are the sins, which lead to death and separation from God, not only in eternity, but now as well. When John says "if anyone sins" he is undoubtedly speaking of those kinds of sins. True Christians will not practice these sins and although they may stumble, they will repent and walk away from them. These sins are not covered by love[79] but must be confronted in love. We are not to ask God whether we should confront these kinds of sins or not. However, there is a sin not leading to death, of which we are all guilty. That is why He says that all unrighteousness is sin. These are things like unkind words, thoughts, impure motives or desires, actions that are unbecoming, coarseness, defensiveness, and on and on. These sins will not necessarily separate us from fellowship with God, but

[79] 1 Pet 4:8

they are not Christ-like and are not pleasing to Him. When we walk in the light, as He is in the light, His blood cleanses us from all sin and unrighteousness. Yet, there is a time when the light of God will expose these flaws in us and expect us to repent and change.

Conclusion

The HG teachers believe they are setting the body of Christ free by their great revelations. They claim to be bringing their followers into a place of rest and peace in the grace of God. However, the fruit that will come from their view of "freedom" will be moral and spiritual shipwreck on the one hand, and deep depression and despair on the other. If Christians believe there is no flesh to contend with or overcome by walking in the power of the Spirit, and no sin to confess and appropriate God's forgiveness for, they have only two options for the way they will live. On the one hand, they will give free reign to the flesh, since they have redefined sin to defang its effect on them spiritually, or they will succumb to condemnation, depression, and doubting their salvation because they know they are not sinless. The devil used these lies to deceive the early Gnostics and now he has repackaged them for the current generation. However, there is no substitute for the true grace of God, which brings us deliverance, and instructs us to deny ungodliness and worldly desires and to live sensibly, righteously and godly in the present age, looking for the blessed hope, and the appearing of the glory of our great God and deliverer, Christ Jesus.[80]

---

[80] Titus 2:11-13

Chapter Five

The Law - Debunking the Myths

Nothing brings out more confusion and contradictions among Christians than a study of the Law of God given through Moses. And much of this confusion is generated by bias and a lack of understanding of Paul's words in Romans and Galatians. We will discuss this in detail later. However, the HG teachers have taken this scholastic mayhem to a completely new level. They have declared war on the Law and intend to expunge all mention of it from the life and teaching of the church. To them it is the cause of all the failure and lack in Christianity down through the ages and must finally be locked away in the vault of Jewish history. It is seen as the opposite of faith, grace, and mercy – a cruel taskmaster that only came to enslave people and show them how wretched they were. Here is a sample of the evidence gathered against it:

"People lived constantly under the awareness of both the severity of the law and their inability to fulfill it! The law was always more of a curse than a blessing to those who were under it! That was its very purpose – to show just how much trouble they were in.... It was given to a people who wanted to do things their own way, as a way to show them they couldn't! It showed them the standard of God's holiness was far beyond anything they could ever hope to achieve themselves. This law was required and yet at the same time wholly impossible to obey. It was meant to drive them to grace and mercy and that grace and mercy could only come through the One who did the impossible by fulfilling the law."[81]

The big problem with this of course is that the Law was given by God and is holy righteous and good. It was a marriage covenant

[81] http://www.phildrysdale.com/2012/10/whats-the-role-of-the-law-in-the-new-covenant/

between Yahweh and His people.[82] We are now supposed to believe that God made a covenant with Israel and locked them into an agreement, which was "wholly impossible for them to obey," and He did this to "drive them to grace." Furthermore, he required that they keep this impossible covenant and because they were unable, He had them butchered by their neighbors and driven from their land for fifteen hundred years. Does this sound like the God of love? Wouldn't it be a better picture of Pharaoh who forced them to make bricks without straw, or Hitler who drove them to ovens because they were Jewish? Consider for a minute the following verses in Deuteronomy:

"These words, which I am commanding you today, shall be on your heart. You shall teach them diligently to your sons and shall talk of them when you sit in your house and when you walk by the way and when you lie down and when you rise up. You shall bind them as a sign on your hand and they shall be as frontals on your forehead. You shall write them on the doorposts of your house and on your gates." Deut 6:6-9

Somehow, these verses do not seem to present the Law as more of a curse than a blessing and something that would bring the people into slavery. On the contrary, they present it as that which gives them freedom. It is a cruel joke to suggest that God was calling the Israelites to write something on their hearts and the hearts of their children that was impossible to obey. What kind of father would do such a thing? Are we to believe that God just wanted them to suffer for fifteen hundred years under laws and statutes that were designed to frustrate them and cause them to fail? Were His promises false since He never told them the Law was impossible to keep? Consider this verse:

"You should diligently keep the commandments of the LORD your God, and His testimonies and His statutes which He has commanded you. You shall do what is right and good in the sight of the LORD, that it may be

---

[82] Jer 31:32

well with you and that you may go in and possess the good land which the LORD swore to give your fathers, by driving out all your enemies from before you, as the LORD has spoken." Deut 6:17-19

Again, God promised that it would go well with them and that He would pour out blessings on them if they kept His commandments. If this Law was wholly impossible to keep, and God knew that, doesn't that make Him a liar? Is God Almighty a liar? Did He trick Israel by commanding them to do something they couldn't do? What kind of husband would demand that His wife do things she could not do and then punish her? Honestly, have these people ever actually studied the Law given by Moses? One has to wonder since they say such things. These are not just false statements - they are an attack on God's character. Consider Yahweh's words to Joshua:

"Only be strong and very courageous; be careful to do according to all the law which Moses My servant commanded you; do not turn from it to the right or to the left, so that you may have success wherever you go. This book of the law shall not depart from your mouth, but you shall meditate on it day and night, so that you may be careful to do according to all that is written in it; for then you will make your way prosperous, and then you will have success. Have I not commanded you? Be strong and courageous! Do not tremble or be dismayed, for the LORD your God is with you wherever you go." Joshua 1:7-9

These wonderful words of comfort to Joshua all hinge on His willingness to keep the Law with all his heart, which of course he did. By the way, Moses also kept the Law with all his heart until his death. Were Joshua and Moses then justified by Law? Not at all. They were justified by their faith and trust in God and because of their faith and trust in God they kept His Law. Therefore, the idea that the Law God gave Israel was impossible to keep is false and it is time the church woke up to this truth. Why then does Paul suggest that the Law was impossible to keep? This idea comes from a misunderstanding of Paul's words, as we shall see. Paul said that no one is justified by the "works of the Law" which is not the same thing. However, before we go there, we must set the stage.

The Missing Ingredient

When we study the Bible, we cannot approach it from the back of the book or from a modern, Gentile perspective. We must read from the beginning forward. The Israelites, according to Paul, were a "cultivated olive tree"[83] as opposed to Gentile believers who were uncultivated. This, of course, refers to the Judaism of his day and not necessarily modern Judaism. They were trained in the Law and the covenants and this training is why they were considered cultivated, or better prepared to understand the New Covenant. Thus, when we read the gospels and the epistles we need to have their perspective if we are to handle difficult concepts accurately. Gentile teachers without this background have caused much confusion because they often misunderstand the very concepts they seek to clarify. For example, when Jesus said that He did not come to "abolish the Law but to fulfill it," what did He mean? Most Bible teachers today will say He came to do away with it or to abolish it. However, they make Jesus contradict Himself and say this instead; "I did not come to abolish the Law but to abolish it." It is amazing to me how many scholarly people will actually say this. Yet here is what Jesus actually said:

"Do not think that I came to abolish the Law or the Prophets; I did not come to abolish but to fulfill. For truly I say to you, until heaven and earth pass away, not the smallest letter or stroke shall pass from the Law until all is accomplished. Whoever then annuls one of the least of these commandments, and teaches others to do the same, shall be called least in the kingdom of heaven; but whoever keeps and teaches them, he shall be called great in the kingdom of heaven." Mt 5:17-19

[83] Rom 11:24

Fulfilling the Law in Jesus' day meant keeping the Law, or walking it out. That is obviously what He was saying. He fulfilled Torah by walking it out perfectly and did not come to eliminate it. Many say that His walking it out perfectly did away with it. However that is again contradicting Jesus' own words for He went on to say that anyone who "annuls one of the least of these commandments, and teaches others to do the same" would be least in the kingdom of heaven. To annul a commandment is to make it invalid. Is it any wonder the HG teachers insist Jesus' teaching does not apply to us, since they not only annul the commandments of the Law; they annul Jesus' commandments as well. Nevertheless, Jesus made portions of the Law obsolete for those in the New Covenant such as the sacrificial system and the civil and dietary laws, but He did not annul or make obsolete the moral teaching of the Law. On the contrary, in the Sermon on the Mount He emphasized it more and challenged us to not only keep it outwardly but in the heart as well. With this, Paul agrees when he says that the righteous requirements of the Law are fulfilled in us who walk according to the Spirit.

Another point that needs to be made is that since Jesus kept the Law perfectly, and the HG teachers agree that He did, then how did He do it? Since many of them also insist that Jesus walked the earth as a man having laid aside His Godhood and the Law was impossible to keep, then how was it possible for Him to do it? Did He keep it as a man or as God? This is another contradiction. However, the Scriptures do not teach that Jesus laid aside His Godhood and ceased to be God as He walked the land of Israel. He laid aside His privileges as God[84]and chose to operate as a man under the power of the Spirit. He was and is the Son of God and He did much that only God could do. Yet, we are commissioned to walk in the same manner as He walked. Why then would we be unable to keep the righteousness requirements of the Law as we walk in the power of the same Holy Spirit?

---

[84] Phil 2:5-9

I realize that some of you want to point out all the apparent negative things Paul and others said about the Law. I promise you we will get to those, but it is imperative that we follow an orderly approach. We cannot understand Paul's words until we understand the subject he was speaking about. This is where we usually go wrong. Besides, reading and studying the Word under the guidance of the Spirit, we must also understand the issues the authors were facing and how they understood things. Therefore, before we discuss the difficult passages concerning the Law in Romans and Galatians, we will first look at the meaning of Paul's terms.

Keys to Romans and Galatians

Romans and Galatians are difficult books. Paul's arguments are challenging even for scholars. He was a man trained in the Hebrew Scriptures and his writings reflect that. Those who lack understanding of First Century Judaism before the advent of Christ will find many of his thoughts impossible to understand. Nevertheless, once we have some of the keys it becomes much easier.

Key #1- The Distortion of Torah/the Law

First of all, Paul was dogged throughout his ministry by the Judaizers. These were believing Jews who insisted that the Gentile converts, such as those in Galatia, had to be circumcised and obey all the Mosaic requirements. They wanted the Gentiles to become Jews as well as Christians, and insisted that they had to comply in order to be fully righteousness. Since the early church was largely Jewish and there was a major Jewish constituency in each local church, this was a big problem. The apostles considered it heresy and it was contrary to the instructions they gave to the churches.[85] These believers operated in the leaven of the Pharisees that Jesus warned His disciples about.[86] They prided themselves in

[85] Acts 15
[86] Mark 8:15

their outward observance of the Law and continued to rely on their "works" even though they were believers in Christ. In Romans, Paul is confronting this and laying the foundation of salvation and justification by faith in Christ and not by works. In Galatians, he is confronting the believers head on because they appear to have succumbed to this heresy.

Another fact that is essential to understanding Paul's discussion in these two letters is his view of the Judaism practiced by the Jews of that period. He understood that God had brought a remnant of Jews into the body of Christ at that time while the nation at large was hardened until the end of the age.[87] He states quite clearly why they were hardened and why they refused to believe in the Messiah.

"*What shall we say then? That Gentiles, who did not pursue righteousness, attained righteousness, even the righteousness which is by faith;* ***but Israel, pursuing a law of righteousness, did not arrive at that law. Why? Because they did not pursue it by faith, but as though it were by works****. They stumbled over the stumbling stone, just as it is written, 'Behold I lay in Zion a stone of stumbling and a rock of offense, and he who believes in Him will not be disappointed.' Brethren, my heart's desire and my prayer to God for them is for their salvation. For I testify about them that they have a zeal for God, but not in accordance with knowledge.* ***For not knowing about God's righteousness and seeking to establish their own, they did not subject themselves to the righteousness of God. For Christ is the end (goal) of the law for righteousness to everyone who believes."*** *Romans 9:30-33, 10:1-4 (Emphasis Mine)*

This statement is a conclusion of Paul's teaching on the Law and Israel in earlier chapters. Israel was given the Law but failed to arrive at that Law or the goal of the Law because they did not pursue it by faith. The nation started in faith but ended up in

[87] Rom 11:25-27

works. They focused on their own effort at keeping the Law and not trusting in the God of Israel. The Law was given as a covenant between them and God but it was never meant to replace their faith in God. It was the means by which they were to present themselves to God based on faith, and not the means by which they were to establish their own righteousness. This was the error of Israel and the distortion of true Judaism and true Law keeping – the kind practiced by the Patriarchs and the prophets of Israel and Jesus Himself. They did not know or acknowledge God's righteousness on the basis of faith, but sought to establish their own through the "works of the Law." Thus, they missed the goal of the Law, which was Christ, and stumbled over the stumbling stone. Jesus confronted this distortion of Judaism throughout His ministry.

"Then Jesus spoke to the crowds and to His disciples, saying: "The scribes and the Pharisees have seated themselves in the chair of Moses; therefore all that they tell you, do and observe, but do not do according to their deeds; for they say things and do not do them.....Woe to you, scribes and Pharisees, hypocrites! For you tithe mint and dill and cummin, and have neglected the weightier provisions of the law: justice and mercy and faithfulness; but these are the things you should have done without neglecting the others. You blind guides, who strain out a gnat and swallow a camel!" Mt 23:1-3, 23-24

Please notice that Jesus did not denounce the teaching of the Pharisees but their practice. They were sticklers about outward observance of the Law but their hearts were not right before God. They were prideful and hypocritical, trusting in their works, and not concerned with faith toward God and the outworking of true righteousness from the heart. They were focused on the works of the Law and observance of the letter of the Law, through which they expected to be justified. Jesus warned His disciples about this mentality or leaven of the Pharisees.[88] However, they were not

[88] Mt 16:8-12

able to remove it from their midst and it became a real problem for the church later on. The Judaizers were infected by the leaven of the Pharisees and they persecuted Paul. This background is very important to understanding Paul's letters and his use of terms such as "under Law," "the letter of the Law," "the works of the Law," etc. These phrases usually denote reliance upon one's own efforts at keeping the Law for justification. This is what we call "legalism." Therefore, as we study the New Testament writings we must bear this in mind. It is especially significant for correct understanding of Romans and Galatians.

Key #2 – The Use of the Article

The understanding of the translators of Scripture often plays a part in the accuracy of their translations. This is not to say that the team of scholars translating the very good and excellent translations we have in English were deliberately inserting bias. On the contrary, by in large they were meticulous in their attempts to keep it out. Yet, sometimes their well-formed theology greatly influenced what they thought the original manuscripts were saying. The use of the Greek article in Romans and Galatians is perhaps the best example of this. Though there is much about the use of the article that can be debated by Greek scholars, nevertheless, the following must be observed:

"It is not necessary for a noun to have the article in order for it to be definite. But conversely, ***a noun cannot be indefinite when it has the article.*** *Thus, it may be definite without the article, and* ***it must be definite with the article****. When a substantive is anarthrous, it may have one of three forces: indefinite, qualitative, or definite."*[89] *(Emphasis Mine)*

Throughout the book of Romans and Galatians, in the original Greek text, the article is usually present when referring to the Law and absent when referring to Legalism. There are some

[89] The Basics of New Testament Syntax: An Intermediate Greek Grammar by Daniel B. Wallace

exceptions when the Law is referred to without the article, however, the translators often put in the article when it does not exist in the Greek and leave it out when it does and its presence is crucial. This is a very puzzling use of the article and seems to favor a specific theology known as Replacement Theology.[90] We will give many examples of this in the next section.

Contrasting Law with Faith

It seems clear that the translators of the best Bibles available today understood Romans and Galatians and other verses concerning the Law from a Replacement Theology mindset. Consequently, they seem to be going out of their way to contrast the Law with Faith and Grace. I do not believe they do this intentionally but since this is their persuasion, it is the only way they can make sense out of the text. The following examples show this in the way they insert or remove the article.

"For I am not ashamed of the gospel, for it is the power of God for salvation to everyone who believes, to the Jew first and also to the Greek. For in it ***the*** *righteousness of God is revealed from faith to faith; as it is written, "BUT THE RIGHTEOUS man SHALL LIVE BY FAITH." Rom 1:16-17 (Emphasis Mine)*

When we say **"The"** righteousness of God is revealed in the gospel message, it implies there has been no righteousness before the gospel. However, the article is not in the Greek and should not have been added. The original says, *"For in it a righteousness of God has been revealed from faith to faith, as it has been written: The righteous man by faith will live."* That is vastly different. What Paul is saying is that a new righteousness has been revealed in the gospel from one faith to another. He affirms that righteousness has always been by faith and not by outward adherence to the Law when he quotes Habakkuk 2:4. In other words, there is a new

---

[90] Replacement Theology is the idea that Israel was replaced by their church and all of her promises now belong to the church.

kind of righteousness revealed from heaven by faith in Messiah for the Jew first and also the Greek. Thus, the idea that before the gospel, righteousness was by law keeping is false. Paul is saying that the Jewish believers have gone from one faith to another – from faith to faith and not from law to faith. The early Jewish believers always viewed faith in the Messiah as "this new faith" or "this faith" or "the faith," as opposed to the old means of faith or trusting God. The same thought occurs in Galatians and is equally distorted by the use of the article.

"But the Scripture has shut up everyone under sin, so that the promise by faith in Jesus Christ might be given to those who believe. But before faith came, we were kept in custody under the law, being shut up to the faith which was later to be revealed. Therefore, the Law has become our tutor to lead us to Christ, so that we may be justified by faith. But now that faith has come, we are no longer under a tutor." Gal 3:22-25

Here the translators leave out the article before the word "faith," which exists in the original, and add the article that does not exist in the original before the word "law." By doing this they convey the idea that faith did not exist during the time of the law and that, it is brand new on the scene. This fits their theology. However, when it comes to the word "law" since in their minds it has to be speaking about "the Law" they add the article. Let us now look at the passage as it actually reads and break it down.

"But the Scripture shut up all men under sin in order that the promise by faith in Jesus the Messiah might be given to the ones believing."

Notice in verse 22 he says the Scripture shut up all men under sin. In verse 23, he says that the Jews were shut up or guarded under law. This same shutting up is summarized in Romans 11 illustrating the harmony of Paul's teaching in both Epistles.

"For just as you (Gentile believers) once were disobedient to God, but now have been shown mercy because of their disobedience (Jews), so these also now have been disobedient, that because of the mercy shown to you they also may now be shown mercy. For God has shut up all in disobedience so that He may show mercy to all." Rom 11:30-32 (Emphasis Mine)

Whereas Galatians 3 says the Scripture and the Law shut up both Jews and Gentiles under sin, Romans 11 says that God shut them up because of their disobedience and that He even used their disobedience as part of His plan to reveal His mercy in Christ. This is the whole point of the early chapters of Romans, which he now summarizes in Chapter 11. The Gentiles, even though they had the witness of creation, and their conscience, did not honor God but worshiped idols and were therefore guilty. The Jews, who had the Law of righteousness given them by God, did not pursue it by faith and instead, tried to establish their own righteousness by a system of legalism by which they were shut up. This is the meaning of the term "under law." And of course this is the meaning of the term in Galatians 3:23 which actually reads like this:

"But before **the** *faith (or this faith) came,* **under law** *(legalism) we were guarded being shut up to* ***the faith*** *about to be revealed." (Emphasis Mine)*

The Jewish Bible puts it this way:

"Now before the time for this trusting faithfulness came, we were imprisoned in subjection to the system which results from perverting the Torah into legalism, kept under guard until this yet-to-come trusting faithfulness would be revealed."[91]

I trust that by now you can see the difference the article makes to our understanding. To say, "When faith came" would no doubt have been insulting to the First Century Jewish believers.

[91] Complete Jewish Bible by David H. Stern, Jewish New Testament Publications, Inc.

Furthermore, it is contradictory to both Romans and Galatians since Paul argues in both that Abraham was justified by his faith prior to the coming of Torah. Now let us proceed to verses 24 and 25 and 26 as they appear in the original.

"Therefore, ***the Law*** *has become our tutor to lead us to Christ, that we may be justified by faith. But now that* ***the faith*** *(or this faith) has come we are no longer under a tutor. For you are all sons of God through* ***the faith*** *in Christ Jesus." Gal 3:24-26 (Emphasis Mine)*

Notice it says that the Law **has become** our tutor or trainer implying that it did not start that way. The Greek word "PAIDAGOGOS" literally means "child conductor." Therefore, the implication is that the Law (the article is in the text) became or was used by God as a child trainer, because of their disobedient and legalistic attitude, to bring them to the place of faith in the Messiah. Now that this faith in Messiah has come, there is no longer any need for the trainer. We are all sons of God through or because of this new faith. The Jewish Bible expresses it beautifully:

"Accordingly, the Torah functioned as a custodian until the Messiah came, so that we might be declared righteous on the ground of trusting and being faithful. But now that the time for this trusting faithfulness has come, we are no longer under a custodian."[92]

Another example of misuse of the article is in Romans 4:13-16:

"For the promise to Abraham or to his descendants that he would be heir of the world was not through the Law, but through the righteousness of faith. For if those who are of the Law are heirs, faith is made void and the promise is nullified; for the Law brings about wrath, but where there is no law, there also is no violation. For this reason it is by faith, in order that it may be in accordance with grace, so that the promise will be guaranteed

[92] Complete Jewish Bible by David H. Stern, Jewish New Testament Publications, Inc.

to all the descendants, not only to those who are of the Law, but also to those who are of the faith of Abraham, who is the father of us all...."Rom 4:13-16

In verse 13, the article is inserted before law and before righteousness obscuring the meaning and suggesting that the Law of God was the opposite of faith and righteousness. Here is how it actually reads:

"For the promise to Abraham or to his descendants that he would be heir of the world was not through Law, but through a righteousness of faith." Verse 13

The phrase "through law" has the same meaning as "the works of the Law." It is the attempt at righteousness by works and not by faith. In other words, the promise to Abraham and his descendants did not come through legalism but through faith. The passage goes on to affirm that the promise is by faith to all the descendants, not only to those who are "of the Law" but also to those "of the faith" of Abraham. The phrase "of the Law" has the same meaning as "through law" and implies works righteousness or legalism. Thus, Paul is saying that the promise is by faith to all Abraham's descendants including those Jews who came out of a system of legalism into faith and those Gentiles who believed by faith. Verses 14 and 15 continue:

"For if those who are of the Law are heirs, faith is made void and the promise is nullified; for the Law brings about wrath, but where there is no law, there also is no violation."

The original NIV[93] does a better job here:
"For if those who live by Law are heirs, faith has no value and the promise is worthless, because law brings wrath. And where there is no law there is no transgression."

---

[93] The NIV has changed much since 1984 as have the other translations.

Those who live by law or literally "out of law" are trying to establish their own righteousness – this is legalism. They are trying to earn righteousness. Thus, if righteousness could be earned, faith would be useless and so would the promise. However, he says that those who trust in their law-keeping receive wrath and punishment rather than a promise because no one can keep the law perfectly. The Jewish Bible expresses it this way.

"For the promise to Avraham and his seed that he would inherit the world did not come through legalism but through the righteousness that trust produces. For if the heirs are produced by legalism, then trust is pointless and the promise worthless. For what law brings is punishment. But where there is no law, there is also no violation. The reason the promise is based on trusting is so that it may come as God's free gift, a promise that can be relied on by all the seed, not only those who live within the framework of the Torah, but also those with the kind of trust Avraham had - Avraham avinu for all of us."

James in his Epistle also addresses the wrath that the Law brings to the legalist:

"If, however, you are fulfilling the royal law according to the Scripture, 'YOU SHALL LOVE YOUR NEIGHBOR AS YOURSELF,' you are doing well. But if you show partiality, you are committing sin and are convicted by the law as transgressors. For whoever keeps the whole law and yet stumbles in one point, he has become guilty of all. For He who said, "DO NOT COMMIT ADULTERY," also said, "DO NOT COMMIT MURDER." Now if you do not commit adultery, but do commit murder, you have become a transgressor of the law. So speak and so act as those who are to be judged by the law of liberty (should be "a law of liberty"). *For judgment will be merciless to one who has shown no mercy; mercy triumphs over judgment." James 2:8-13*

Here James is confronting an attitude of favoritism toward the rich among Jewish believers who follow the Law (Torah). He scolds them for their hypocrisy in claiming to keep the Law and yet breaking it by their attitude. He outlines the futility of legalism in that no one can keep the Law perfectly, because we all stumble, and that legalism is without mercy. He admonishes them to live by the heart of the Law or what he calls the royal law, which is summed up by the command to "love your neighbor as yourself."[94] He exhorts them to live by "a law of liberty," which will judge them and not a system of legalism. Again, the Jewish Bible expresses it beautifully:

"If you truly attain the goal of Kingdom Torah, in conformity with the passage that says, "Love your neighbor as yourself," you are doing well. But if you show favoritism, your actions constitute sin, since you are convicted under the Torah as transgressors. For a person who keeps the whole Torah, yet stumbles at one point, has become guilty of breaking them all. For the One who said, 'Don't commit adultery,'also said, 'Don't murder.' Now, if you don't commit adultery but do murder, you have become a transgressor of the Torah. Keep speaking and acting like people who will be judged by a Torah which gives freedom. For judgment will be without mercy toward one who doesn't show mercy; but mercy wins out over judgment."

The Law Came to Increase Sin?

"The purpose of the law was to increase sin. (Romans 5:20) The law makes you sinful beyond measure. (Romans 7:13)"[95]

The above statements are deeply troubling and are not only dead wrong, but they reveal a deep-seated anger or even hatred toward the Law. However, they are a good representation of what the "HG" teachers and many in the church have been teaching.

---

[94] Lev 19:18
[95] http://www.phildrysdale.com/2012/10/whats-the-role-of-the-law-in-the-new-covenant/

However, is this really the purpose of the Law – to increase sin? Does the law actually make you sinful? Let's take a look at the above mentioned passages and see what they actually say.

"So then as through one transgression there resulted condemnation to all men, even so through one act of righteousness there resulted justification of life to all men. For as through the one man's disobedience the many were made sinners, even so through the obedience of the One the many will be made righteous. ***The Law came in so that the transgression would increase; but where sin increased, grace abounded all the more****, so that, as sin reigned in death, even so grace would reign through righteousness to eternal life through Jesus Christ our Lord. What shall we say then? Are we to continue in sin so that grace may increase? May it never be! How shall we who died to sin still live in it?" Rom 5:18-2, 6:1-2 (Emphasis Mine)*

To take this verse (Rom 5:20) out of context and suggest it means that the purpose of the Law was to increase sin is utter foolishness. Does God initiate sin? Did He desire to see more people sinning? Did He give the Law so that there would be more wickedness? Heaven forbid! What Paul is saying here has to be kept in the context of what he has said earlier and put together with the other passages. He realizes that some will interpret his words this way and addresses it in chapter 6:1, "Are we to continue in sin that grace might increase?" The answer of course is, "May it never be," or as we would say, "Heaven forbid." Therefore, to understand the statement, "the law came that transgression might increase," we must go back to chapter 5, verse 13.

"…For until the Law sin was in the world; but sin is not imputed where there is no law." Rom 5:13

Before the Law came, there was plenty of sin. From the time of Adam until Noah, mankind became more and more sinful. In fact, so much so, that God's heart was grieved and He was sorry he made man.[96] The result was that He wiped mankind of the face of the earth preserving Noah and His family to begin again. So it is clear that sin was in the world, increasing from one generation to another as it does today. What is the point then? Does the introduction of the Law cause sin to increase? It does in a technical sense since sins overlooked by God prior to the Law were now charged against the people. An illustration would be as follows:

A group of toddlers are left alone in the nursery and no one is watching them. Soon they are having a great time tearing the room apart, throwing things, biting each other and so on. They are doing all this because of their sinful nature. You can be certain that they will not act with respect for others or leave the room in an orderly fashion. Nevertheless, when an adult is appointed to attend to them he or she will have to do something about the chaos. The adult will introduce a set of rules that will restore order to the nursery. The list might include, "no more biting," "no pulling hair," "share the toys," "put all the toys back when you are finished," etc. With each violation of the rules a penalty is added. These days it usually means kids are sent back to their parents if they are misbehaving. In this way the children are protected, the parents are happy, and we are on the road to raising godly children who will also raise godly children using the same rules. Now, was there sin in the toddler room before the rules came? As they say up north, "You betcha." Was there more sin after the rules came? The answer is actually yes. You may ask, "How can that be?" Because, before the rules came, no one was keeping track and there was no punishment and the kids were not aware of how bad their behavior was. But now since there are rules and supervision, and the kids know that they are doing wrong, there is more sin being recorded and thus more sinning taking place. Also, there is more rebellion since the old rebel

---

[96] Gen 6:6

nature in the children is being challenged resulting in more attitudes, temper tantrums, manipulation, etc. Yet, the system of rules is bringing more order to the church and the children are learning to value and obey the rules because of the consequences if they do not. Thus, the children are being protected from absolute mayhem and destruction and a legacy is preserved.

The above illustration is an attempt to explain the purpose of the Law as presented by the apostle Paul. (I am speaking in human terms as he did.[97]) Obviously, no one in their right mind would suggest that the nursery should have no supervision and no rules. However, the rules themselves cannot change the children but only show them their rebellion and where they must change. It is true that the Law stirs up the rebel in us,[98] but it is also true that it shows us our rebellion and gives us a chance to humble ourselves and receive His grace to change.

Let us now look at the second reference quoted above:

"The law makes you sinful beyond measure. (Romans 7:13)"[99]

The above statement is a serious twisting of Romans 7:13. It does not say that the Law **makes** you sinful beyond measure. In fact, it says the opposite.

"Therefore ***did that which is good become a cause of death for me? May it never be!*** *Rather it was sin, in order that it might be shown to be sin by effecting my death through that which is good, so that* ***through the commandment sin would become utterly sinful****."* *Rom 7:13 (Emphasis Mine)*

[97] Rom 6:19

[98] Rom 7:5

[99]http://www.phildrysdale.com/2012/10/whats-the-role-of-the-law-in-the-new-covenant/

Paul is here concluding that it is not the Law that is the problem but us. The commandment exposes the sinful nature in us, which is utterly sinful. The commandment was not the cause of death but the sinful nature. Notice how he distinguishes between the body of the Law and "the commandment." This is something Gentiles unaccustomed to First Century Jewish thinking would not get.

The term "The Law" is used to speak of the whole body of Torah including the commandments, sacrificial system of forgiveness and punishment, etc. However, sometimes it is also used to speak of one aspect. In this case, Paul is specific. It is the commandment that stirs up the rebel nature. For instance, when a child is told not to do something, like, "Don't touch the cookies on the counter," his eyes immediately look toward the counter. Now that he is aware of the commandment, his desire to get the cookies increases. In this way, the commandment arouses sin, because before it came, touching the cookies was not known to be a sin. Let us now look at Romans 7:13 again, this time keeping it together with the preceding verses.

"What shall we say then? Is the Law sin? May it never be! On the contrary, I would not have come to know sin except through the Law; for I would not have known about coveting if the Law had not said, "YOU SHALL NOT COVET." But sin, taking opportunity ***through the commandment****, produced in me coveting of every kind; for apart from the Law sin is dead. I was once alive apart from the Law; but* ***when the commandment came****, sin became alive and I died;* ***and this commandment****, which was to result in life, proved to result in death for me;* ***for sin, taking an opportunity through the commandment,*** *deceived me and through it killed me. So then, the Law is holy,* ***and the commandment is holy and righteous and good.*** *Therefore did that which is good become a cause of death for me? May it never be!* ***Rather it was sin****, in order that it might be shown to be sin by effecting my death through that which is good, so that* ***through the***

commandment sin would become utterly sinful**.**" *Rom 7:7-13 (Emphasis Mine)*

The point here is that the commandment challenges the rebel sinful nature and exposes it. Paul is not blaming the Law for the sin but illustrating that it is our sinful nature that is the problem and it was there before the Law. Therefore, the purpose of the Law was not to make Israel more sinful, but to teach and train the people and preserve them as a nation until the Messiah came. Paul expressed it this way:

"Why the Law then? It was added ***because of transgressions****, having been ordained through angels by the agency of a mediator,* ***until the seed would come to whom the promise had been made****." Gal 3:19 (Emphasis Mine)*

When we consider the nation that was brought out of Egypt and compare them with their ancestors Jacob and Joseph, we can see clearly the progression of sin in each generation. The people have strayed from the values of their forefathers and have become like the Canaanites in the land. This is the reason the Law was given – because of transgressions. When God appeared to the Israelites in glory on Mount Sinai the people were very frightened. They trembled and stood at a distance and pleaded with Moses to go before God on his own and bring back the word to them. Then Moses said to them:

"Do not be afraid; for God has come in order to test you, and in order that the fear of Him may remain with you, so that you may not sin." Ex 20:20

Whenever humans encounter the glory of God, they generally experience great delight and great fear. This is true in the New Testament[100] as well as the Old. Moses told the people that God wanted them to fear Him so they would not sin. Then He made a

[100] Rev 1:17, Acts 5:11

covenant with them giving them the Law, which revealed His righteous requirements and the sacrificial system as a means of forgiveness, although some sins could not be forgiven and required the penalty of death. Many in the church today find this hard to accept. Yet, even in our sophisticated, 'progressive' Western nations we must execute justice and lock people away in prisons. What is often forgotten is that the Old Covenant not only regulated the Israelites relationship with God, it also of necessity administered civil justice. Nevertheless, despite the fact that Israel rebelled against God repeatedly, the Law preserved them as a nation "until the seed would come through whom the promise had been made."

Difficult Passages

There is no question that the subject of the Law is difficult to understand and explain. Countless Jewish sages have given their lives to study it and meditate on its mysteries including the Biblical prophets and apostles. Paul, who was a brilliant scholar who studied under the famous Rabbi Gamaliel, is not always easy to understand, particularly as he teaches us concerning the Law. Though his writings are in Greek he thought in Hebrew and frequently used idioms of speech and Jewish Midrash, which are unknown to 21st Century Gentiles. Because of this, his writings are often misunderstood and distorted by the ignorant and unstable.[101]

Today, pastors and leaders are quick to spout on about how they "got a revelation" of this and that. Sometimes their "revelations" are good and sometimes they are plain wrong and create more confusion. Though I always seek and receive revelation from God as I study Scripture, revelation is not enough. Our revelation must be tested with real scholarship. God is not going to do the studying for us. He expects us to meditate and pour over His word. In addition, what we discover must be in harmony with the

---

[101] 2Pet 3:15-16

whole body of Scripture, no matter how significant the dream or vision. Therefore, if we are ever going to understand the difficult passages we must understand the thoughts of the writer who was inspired by the Spirit. We must take the time to study what he studied and understand his worldview. Otherwise, we will come away with a distorted or incomplete picture.

Another factor that greatly affects modern interpretation of the New Testament writings is the attitude toward the Hebrew Scriptures that has existed in the church for centuries, and has gone viral in our day. It began in the 2nd Century with the rejection of the Jews and mushroomed into full-blown hatred of anything Jewish, even in the Bible. Then in the 3rd and 4th centuries, it was enshrined in the doctrine of Replacement Theology, where the Old Testament was sanitized with all of the passages and promises that were good applied to the church. Since that time there has been a tendency to not only look at the Law as being old and obsolete, but the Hebrew Scriptures as well. Indeed, the term "Old Testament" was wrongly applied to the first thirty seven books of the Bible, rather than merely the Mosaic covenant. As we have already noted, certain aspects of the Law are obsolete in the New Covenant, but the moral Law is not. However, when one views all of the Hebrew Scriptures as the "Old Testament" it is hard to avoid the conclusion that it is all obsolete and not authoritative in our lives. This is, of course, the common approach to the Bible today and especially that of the "Grace Revolution." In their minds, the Old Testament is the Law – the system we have been liberated from. Thus, anything that they don't like is relegated to "Old Testament Law Keeping." It is this root more than any other that has led to this current crisis – and it is a crisis. However, sadly it is not exclusive to them. It has been around for some time, throughout the Twentieth Century and in the Revival movement, which tends to disdain theology, it has found a fertile field.

This attitude toward the Old Testament that is rooted in Replacement Theology leads believers to the conclusion that there was no grace or faith in the Old Covenant. However, nothing could be further from the truth. I remember as a young Christian being taught that in the New Covenant our hearts were circumcised, whereas in the Old Covenant it was just outward circumcision in the flesh. Later on, I would discover that heart circumcision was actually an Old Testament concept. God challenged the people to be circumcised in heart and not just the flesh,[102] and the prophets echoed that theme in their warnings to Israel.[103] However, the church comes to such erroneous conclusions because of an existing bias toward the Old Testament.

Another one of those conclusions is that there was no grace in the Law, even in the Old Testament period. This is a monumental error. Though there were clearly sins that could not be forgiven in the Levitical system, there was also much grace and forgiveness extended to the people. When we read the list of sundry laws, it can sound heartless and even overwhelming, but the detail is filled with mercy and care for the poor and oppressed and the preservation of life and happiness among the people. So much so that the New Testament writers, including Christ Himself, were able to sum it up in the commandments to love God and our neighbor.[104] Yet, today's church cannot see any love at all in the Law and the reason is simple - they don't want to.

Another tragic error of modern Christianity is the assumption that the Old Testament and the Law were not about faith. This idea comes more from an attitude toward Biblical Judaism than from the study of Scripture. Again, nothing could be further from the truth. The laws and sacrifices were for repentance and cleansing from sin and relationship with God, and some of them were just

---

[102] Lev 26:41

[103] Jer 9:26, Ezek 44:7-9

[104] Mt 22:37-40, Rom 13:8-10, James 2:8

about fellowshipping with God. However, the notion that they were to be justified by their works is false. They were expected to do all these things because of their faith in God and their love for Him. The fact that the people began to relate to the Law in a legalistic way and attempt to establish their own righteousness apart from faith, does not invalidate the Law or suggest that it was impossible to follow. Indeed, we know that many Old Testament saints did exactly that. Furthermore, to suggest that this is not so, is to miss the whole point and argue with Scripture itself. It is also to suggest that Moses, Joshua, David, Isaiah, Jeremiah, Ezekiel, Daniel and a host of others were legalists and did not walk by faith because they kept the Old Covenant. Consider these passages from the prophets:

"'What are your multiplied sacrifices to Me?' says the LORD. 'I have had enough of burnt offerings of rams and the fat of fed cattle; and I take no pleasure in the blood of bulls, lambs or goats. "When you come to appear before Me, who requires of you this trampling of My courts? Bring ***your worthless offerings*** *no longer, incense is an abomination to Me. New moon and sabbath, the calling of assemblies -I cannot endure iniquity and the solemn assembly. I hate your new moon festivals and your appointed feasts, they have become a burden to Me; I am weary of bearing them. So when you spread out your hands in prayer, I will hide My eyes from you; yes, even though you multiply prayers, I will not listen. Your hands are covered with blood. Wash yourselves, make yourselves clean; remove the evil of your deeds from My sight. Cease to do evil, learn to do good; seek justice, reprove the ruthless, defend the orphan, plead for the widow. Come now, and let us reason together,' says the LORD, 'Though your sins are as scarlet, they will be as white as snow; though they are red like crimson, they will be like wool. If you consent and obey, you will eat the best of the land; but if you refuse and rebel, you will be devoured by the sword. Truly, the mouth of the LORD has spoken." Is 1:11-20 (Emphasis Mine)*

Perhaps there is no more impassioned plea in all of Scripture for the people to come to God with their hearts right before Him than this one. God says their sacrifices are worthless because their hearts are not in it and they are walking by legalism and not by faith.

"Because this people draw near with their words and honor Me with their lip service, but they remove their hearts far from Me, ***and their reverence for Me consists of tradition learned by rote."*** *Is 29:13 (Emphasis Mine)*

Could there be a better description of Legalism than this? Jesus Himself quoted these verses and applied them to the self-righteous legalism into which Israel had fallen.[105] They were doing all the outward stuff by rote, trusting in their own works for righteousness and having a stony heart toward God.

"Keep on listening, but do not perceive; keep on looking, but do not understand. Render the hearts of this people insensitive, their ears dull, and their eyes dim, otherwise they might see with their eyes, hear with their ears, understand with their hearts, and return and be healed." Is 6:8-10

"And rend your heart and not your garments. Now return to the LORD your God, for He is gracious and compassionate, slow to anger, abounding in lovingkindness and relenting of evil." Joel 2:13

It is clear from these and many other passages that the prophets of Israel did not live in legalism. Indeed, throughout Israel's history there was always a remnant that walked by faith and kept the commandments as an expression of their love for God. Furthermore, they constantly confronted the legalistic approach of living by works. With this in mind, let us now look at some of the more difficult passages of the New Testament regarding the Law and attempt to explain their correct meaning.

---

[105] Mt 13:14-16,

"The law frustrates grace. (Galatians 2:21)"[106]
"The law has nothing to do with faith." (Galatians 3:11-12)[107]
"The law was a curse that Christ redeemed us from." (Galatians 3:13)[108]

The above quotes are a complete distortion of Paul's teaching in the book of Galatians. Without the knowledge that the apostle is confronting a legalistic approach to the Law, and not the Law itself, he is made to say the opposite of what he actually does say. However, in order to get to the truth we will put these verses back in context and look at the passage as a whole. I have placed the article in parentheses when it does not appear in the original.

"We are Jews by nature and not sinners from among the Gentiles; nevertheless knowing that ***a man is not justified by the works of (the) Law but through faith in Christ Jesus****, even we have believed in Christ Jesus, so that we may be justified by faith in Christ and* ***not by the works of (the) Law; since by the works of (the) Law no flesh will be justified.*** *But if, while seeking to be justified in Christ, we ourselves have also been found sinners, is Christ then a minister of sin? May it never be! For if I rebuild what I have once destroyed, I prove myself to be a transgressor. For through (the) Law I died to (the) Law, so that I might live to God. I have been crucified with Christ; and it is no longer I who live, but Christ lives in me; and the life which I now live in the flesh I live by faith in the Son of God, who loved me and gave Himself up for me.* ***I do not nullify the grace of God, for if righteousness comes through (the) Law, then Christ died needlessly."*** *Gal 2:15-21(Emphasis Mine)*

Paul is actually relating how he admonished Peter when he came to Antioch and was eating freely with the Gentiles until certain Jews came from Jerusalem. Then Peter began to withdraw and

---

[106] http://www.phildrysdale.com/2012/10/whats-the-role-of-the-law-in-the-new-covenant/
[107] http://www.phildrysdale.com/2012/10/whats-the-role-of-the-law-in-the-new-covenant/
[108] http://www.phildrysdale.com/2012/10/whats-the-role-of-the-law-in-the-new-covenant/

hold himself aloof because he was afraid of the "party of the circumcision." In other words, Peter, who believed that he was free in Christ to eat with the Gentiles, went back to a works system of righteousness out of fear. Paul is confronting him because of his hypocrisy and reminding him that no one can be justified by the "works of law" or legalistic observance of Torah. He goes on to imply that Peter was building up the legalistic system, which had been preventing the Jews from receiving Messiah, and in this way rebuilding what he once destroyed. He reaffirms that he has been crucified with Christ and has died to legalism and works righteousness, and now lives his life by faith in, or by the faith of, the son of God – this new faith in Messiah. He declares that going back to legalism or the "works of the law" for righteousness actually nullifies, or sets aside, the grace of God and makes Christ's death needless. In other words, if we can earn righteousness by our own effort at keeping the Law, then there is no need for faith.

Paul is not saying that the Law of God frustrates grace but the system of legalism, developed by the Jews in their attempt to establish their own righteousness, frustrates and nullifies grace. Then he turns his attention to the Galatians because they had begun to turn to trusting in "legalistic observance of the Law" for righteousness and had succumbed to the message of the Judaizers.
"You foolish Galatians, who has bewitched you, before whose eyes Jesus Christ was publicly portrayed as crucified? This is the only thing I want to find out from you: did you receive the Spirit ***by the works of the Law****, or by hearing with faith? Are you so foolish? Having begun by the Spirit, are you now being perfected by the flesh? Did you suffer so many things in vain - if indeed it was in vain? So then, does He who provides you with the Spirit and works miracles among you,* ***do it by the works of the Law****, or by hearing with faith?" Gal 3:1-5(Emphasis Mine)*
The Galatians came into the glorious freedom of Christ being made righteous by their faith in Him. But now they are being bewitched, deceived by the controlling Judaizers who are teaching

them that they must be circumcised and obey all of the ceremonial laws in order to be considered truly righteous before God. This of course is a betrayal of Christ since they are already righteous because of their faith in Him. It is also a betrayal of the counsel of the apostles and elders of the church.[109] Then Paul asks them if they received the Holy Spirit because they heard the message of the gospel and responded in faith, or if they had earned the Holy Spirit though their meticulous law keeping. Then he scolds them, "Are you so foolish? Having begun by the Spirit are you now being perfected by the flesh?" Since they received the Spirit by faith or trust in the gospel message, he wants to know why they think they can now come to maturity or perfection based on their own efforts at keeping the Law. Notice, Paul considers this legalism a work of the flesh. This echoes his words in Romans 7:5, where he recalls his life in Judaism as being in the flesh.[110] Please remember that legalism is not only a distortion of Christianity but Biblical Judaism as well. Nevertheless, Paul goes on in verses 6-9, as he does in Romans 4, to speak about how Abraham was justified by faith before Torah came, and that those who are justified by faith are his true descendants. Then he goes on to declare that legalists are under a curse.

"For as many as are of the works of (the) Law are under a curse; for it is written, "CURSED IS EVERYONE WHO DOES NOT ABIDE BY ALL THINGS WRITTEN IN THE BOOK OF THE LAW, TO PERFORM THEM." Gal 3:10

Here Paul takes a direct swipe at the Judaizers who are "of" the works of the Law. It is not that they are so compliant with the teaching of Torah, but that they are operating in the flesh, trusting in their own righteousness, which they believe they receive through the flesh and human effort. He says this puts them under a curse and he quotes Deuteronomy 27:26 which recounts the curses pronounced on Mt. Ebal. The insertion of this verse causes

---

[109] Acts 15:28-29

[110] Rom 7:5

people to assume Paul is affirming legalism as God's intent in Torah. However, this is not at all what he is saying. God never required absolute perfection from the people in their keeping of all of his commands and statutes. He was not frustrating or exasperating them with laws they couldn't keep. There was mercy and forgiveness in the sacrificial system to cover their weakness and failures.

Paul is using Deuteronomy 27:26 in the same way the Judaizers used it. They are the ones who treat the Law as a matter of legalistic observance. They have reduced it to a list of rules, which they perform by rote crediting righteousness to themselves. This approach is an affront to God since it is not from the heart and is not from faith and love. Thus, the apostle is reminding them that this attitude brings them under a curse because if they don't keep everything perfectly, they will be guilty of all. Notice he says, it is those who are "of the works of law" that are under a curse, not every Torah abiding Jew.

"Now that no one is justified by (the) Law before God is evident; for, "THE RIGHTEOUS MAN SHALL LIVE BY FAITH." However, the Law is not of faith; on the contrary, "HE WHO PRACTICES THEM SHALL LIVE BY THEM." Gal 3:11-12

He has already stated clearly that no human being is justified before God by his works.[111] Now he says it again quoting Habakkuk 2:4. This is the same argument as in Romans 1:17. He is making it clear that in the Old Covenant, as well as the New, the righteous always live by faith and not by legalism. Nothing else has ever been acceptable to God. No one can be justified by going through the outward motions only. His heart must be in it and thus there must be a response of faith. Then he says, "The Law is not of faith." This statement has to be kept in its context to be understood. It is not the Law itself that is being referenced, but this legalistic approach to it. This is evidenced by the quote from

---

[111] Gal 2:16

Leviticus 18:5, which follows, *"He who practices them shall live by them."* As with Deuteronomy 27:26, this quote from the Law is being used to show the futility of legalism. In other words, there are two approaches to the Law the legalistic approach and the faith approach. If you choose the faith approach, you live in the Law the way it was intended to be lived. However, if you follow the legalistic approach, and trust in your own works, the curses in the Law will come upon you, because even if you could keep everything perfectly in an outward sense, you would still be violating the heart of the Law.

"Now, Israel, what does the LORD your God require from you, but to fear the LORD your God, ***to walk in all His ways and love Him,*** *and to serve the LORD your God* ***with all your heart and with all your soul****, and to keep the LORD'S commandments and His statutes which I am commanding you today for your good? Behold, to the LORD your God belong heaven and the highest heavens, the earth and all that is in it. Yet on your fathers did the LORD set His affection to love them, and He chose their descendants after them, even you above all peoples, as it is this day.* ***So circumcise your heart,*** *and stiffen your neck no longer." Deut 10:12-16 (Emphasis Mine)*

Notice that keeping God's commandments is to be a response of love and faith from the heart and not some outward legalistic exercise. This is the way the godly men of old approached the Law. It is also the way Jesus Himself kept the Law perfectly and confronted the legalistic approach condemning it as hypocrisy. And because He was free of the legalistic approach He was able to take the curse contained in Torah on Himself.

Christ redeemed us from the curse of the Law, having become a curse for us - for it is written, "CURSED IS EVERYONE WHO HANGS ON A TREE" - in order that in Christ Jesus the blessing of Abraham might come to the Gentiles, so that we would receive the promise of the Spirit through (the or this) [112] *faith." Gal 3:10-14*

Notice Paul says, "Christ redeemed **us,**" meaning those Jews who were operating in legalism by taking the curse contained in the Law on Himself. He goes back to Deuteronomy, this time chapter 21 verse 23 to illustrate this. By hanging on a tree Jesus bore the curses due the Jews for their breaking of the Law and also opened the way for the Gentiles, who were also under a curse because of sin, to receive the promise of Abraham by faith. Then he says, "in order that we," both Jews and Gentiles, would receive the promise of the Spirit by **this** faith. Again, the translators have wrongly omitted the article, which occurs in the Greek, thus misleading the reader to think that faith did not exist before Christ came.

A parallel passage to Galatians 3:10-14 is found in Romans 10:1-10 and it is equally difficult to understand without some background.

"Brethren, my heart's desire and my prayer to God for them is for their salvation. For I testify about them that they have a zeal for God, but not in accordance with knowledge. For not knowing about God's righteousness and seeking to establish their own, they did not subject themselves to the righteousness of God. For Christ is the end of the law for righteousness to everyone who believes. For Moses writes that the man who practices the righteousness which is based on law shall live by that righteousness. But the righteousness based on faith speaks as follows: 'DO NOT SAY IN YOUR HEART, "WHO WILL ASCEND INTO HEAVEN?" (that is, to bring Christ down), or "WHO WILL DESCEND INTO THE ABYSS?" (that is, to bring Christ up from the dead)." But what does it say? 'THE WORD IS NEAR YOU, IN YOUR MOUTH AND IN YOUR HEART'—that is, the word of faith which we are preaching, that if you confess with your mouth Jesus as Lord, and believe in your heart that God raised Him from the dead, you will be saved; for with the

---

[112] Though not in the Translation the article is in the Greek. It is "through this faith."

heart a person believes, resulting in righteousness, and with the mouth he confesses, resulting in salvation." Rom 10:1-10

Paul expresses his great burden for the Jewish people and for their salvation throughout chapter 9 and 10. He says they have a zeal for God but they are without knowledge since they have become ensnared in legalism and are trying to establish their own righteousness through works. This is the reason he gives for their inability to accept the righteousness of God in the Messiah. Christ is the goal of the Law, but they have been unable to come to Christ because of their reliance upon works. They have stumbled over the stumbling stone. Then he goes on to compare the legalistic approach to righteousness and the faith approach by using the words of Moses. He compares the way the legalists apply Moses to the faith approach given by Moses himself. This distinction is not discernable without an understanding of First Century Judaism and the insight of Paul who was a Hebrew of Hebrews. Thus when Gentile Christians who don't have this background read the passage they think that Paul is contrasting the Law with faith, when in fact he is not doing that at all. Here is what he says:

"For Moses writes that the man who practices the righteousness which is based on law shall live by that righteousness. ***But the righteousness based on faith*** *speaks as follows…." (Emphasis Mine)*

He quotes Moses as the legalists interpret him – the man who practices the righteousness based on or out of law. That is a perfect description of a legalist. The reference may be Leviticus 18:5. The legalists claim that strict outward observance of the commandments makes a person righteous and this they attempted to do without faith and the inner repentance of the heart also required by the Law. Thus, they distorted the Law and made it merely a system of works. Paul contrasts this approach with faith – the faith approach that he also quotes from the Law. This time he references Deuteronomy 30:11-14. Notice he is not contrasting the Law itself with faith as many teachers incorrectly assume. He is contrasting the works righteousness approach that Israel had adopted, with the true teaching of Moses. He quotes Moses as also having said that the word was near them, in their heart and in their mouth and not too difficult to keep. Thus, Moses is also the source of the faith approach, which is the correct approach to God's word.

"But the righteousness based on faith speaks as follows: 'DO NOT SAY IN YOUR HEART, "WHO WILL ASCEND INTO HEAVEN?" (that is, to bring Christ down), or "WHO WILL DESCEND INTO THE ABYSS?" (that is, to bring Christ up from the dead)." But what does it say? 'THE WORD IS NEAR YOU, IN YOUR MOUTH AND IN YOUR HEART'"

This is a direct quote from Deuteronomy 30 but Paul substitutes Christ and the word of Christ for the command of Torah. He is making the point that the word of faith, which he is preaching, must be received in the heart and confessed with the mouth resulting in true God given righteousness.

"But what does it say? 'THE WORD IS NEAR YOU, IN YOUR MOUTH AND IN YOUR HEART'—that is, the word of faith which we are preaching, that if you confess with your mouth Jesus as Lord, and believe in your heart that God raised Him from the dead, you will be saved; for with the heart a person believes, resulting in righteousness, and with the mouth he confesses, resulting in salvation."

This whole passage is intended to show the foolishness of legalism and reliance on works, which had become the practice of the Jewish nation rather than an attitude of faith and trust.

The Law Put Israel in Slavery

"The law makes you a slave like Hagar. (Galatians 4:24)"[113]

The above statement is another disastrous distortion but since most believers think this way, they will shout "Amen." However, to say that the Law itself makes one a slave is to say that God brought Israel into slavery at Sinai. This is an absurd conclusion since God brought them "out of the house of slavery."[114] Surely, this is not what Paul had in mind when he wrote this passage? Yet, it is the conclusion of those who casually read the text or who do not have the background to understand what the apostle was really saying. Galatians is a difficult book and this is perhaps the most difficult passage in it, yet it must be put together with the rest of Scripture. It cannot be made to say something that is contrary to other passages. Paul's terminology must be understood as well as the issues he is addressing. Besides, in other passages he has made it clear that the Law itself is not the cause of Israel's slavery but their self-righteous attitude toward it. In view of this, let us examine this passage in Gal 4, quoting it first and then breaking it down.

"*Tell me, you who want to be under law, do you not listen to the law? For it is written that Abraham had two sons, one by the bondwoman and one by the free woman. But the son by the bondwoman was born according to the flesh, and the son by the free woman through the promise. This is allegorically speaking, for these women are two covenants: one proceeding from Mount Sinai bearing children who are to be slaves; she is Hagar. Now this Hagar is Mount Sinai in Arabia and corresponds to the present Jerusalem, for she is in slavery with her children. But the Jerusalem above is free; she is our mother. For it is written, 'REJOICE, BARREN WOMAN WHO DOES NOT BEAR; BREAK FORTH AND SHOUT, YOU WHO ARE NOT IN LABOR; FOR MORE NUMEROUS ARE THE CHILDREN OF THE*

---

[113]http://www.phildrysdale.com/2012/10/whats-the-role-of-the-law-in-the-new-covenant/
[114] Exodus 13:3

DESOLATE THAN OF THE ONE WHO HAS A HUSBAND.' And you brethren, like Isaac, are children of promise. But as at that time he who was born according to the flesh persecuted him who was born according to the Spirit, so it is now also. But what does the Scripture say? 'CAST OUT THE BONDWOMAN AND HER SON, FOR THE SON OF THE BONDWOMAN SHALL NOT BE AN HEIR WITH THE SON OF THE FREE WOMAN.' So then, brethren, we are not children of a bondwoman, but of the free woman." Gal 4:21-31

Paul addressed this section to those who have embraced legalism. We have seen already that the phrase "under law" means legalism.

"*Tell me, you who want to be under law, do you not listen to the law?*

He confronts those who apparently want to be under a legalistic system by asking them if they listen to the Law itself. Then he goes on to quote from Genesis which most Christians would not even consider to be part of the Law. However, from the Hebrew mindset, "the Law" was a term used to speak of more than the Commandments themselves. Here it is being used with reference to the Five Books of Moses – the Torah. Other times it is used of the Torah and the oral traditions, something that Jews were able to distinguish. In any event, He goes on to talk about Sarah and Hagar and Isaac and Ishmael.

"For it is written that Abraham had two sons, one by the bondwoman and one by the free woman. But the son by the bondwoman was born according to the flesh, and the son by the free woman through the promise."

Abraham had two sons, one from the slave Hagar the Egyptian, whose name was Ishmael, and the other from Sarah, his wife, whose name was Isaac. Isaac was the son of the promise of God and his birth was supernatural, whereas Ishmael was a result of Abraham's attempt to fulfill God's promise on his own strength. Thus, he was "of the flesh." Then Paul presents what in Judaism is known as a Midrash – a story or an allegory to make a point.

*"**This is allegorically speaking**, for these women are two covenants: one proceeding from Mount Sinai bearing children **who are to be** slaves; she is Hagar. Now this Hagar is Mount Sinai in Arabia and corresponds to the present Jerusalem, for she is in slavery with her children. But the Jerusalem above is free; she is our mother."*

Paul makes it very clear that the next thing he is about to say is not to be taken literally. He is speaking allegorically with regard to Sarah and Hagar by comparing them to Sinai and the Jerusalem above. In other words, he wants to make a point with an illustration and not speak against the Law. Notice he says that the children of the covenant from Sinai became slaves. They became slaves because they rebelled against God and abused and distorted the Law. He says they are now enslaved in the earthly Jerusalem, both physically by the Romans and spiritually because of their legalistic system of righteousness. Thus, those who are under law are enslaved while those who are in the Jerusalem above (presumably the New Jerusalem) are free. The Messiah is above and so are all those saints who have experienced His deliverance. In other words, our hope and promise is in the city above and not in the earthly city. Then he quotes from Isaiah 54:

"For it is written, 'REJOICE, BARREN WOMAN WHO DOES NOT BEAR; BREAK FORTH AND SHOUT, YOU WHO ARE NOT IN LABOR; FOR MORE NUMEROUS ARE THE CHILDREN OF THE DESOLATE THAN OF THE ONE WHO HAS A HUSBAND.'"

Isaiah 54 is about the restoration of Israel and the coming kingdom of the Messiah. This is the promise that the early believers and we also are waiting for. Thus, we are children of the promise – the offspring of the Holy Spirit and not the flesh. Consequently the admonition:

*"And **you brethren, like Isaac, are children of promise**. But as at that time he who was born according to the flesh persecuted him who was born according to the Spirit, so it is now also. But what does the Scripture*

say? 'CAST OUT THE BONDWOMAN AND HER SON, for THE SON OF THE BONDWOMAN SHALL NOT BE AN HEIR WITH THE SON OF THE FREE WOMAN.' So then, brethren, we are not children of a bondwoman, but of the free woman." Gal 4:21-31(Emphasis Mine)

Isaac, who was the son of the promise, was persecuted by the child of the flesh (Ishmael) and still is to this day. In the same way, the legalists who represent those who walk by the flesh persecute those of us who are born of the Spirit. Therefore, we must cast out the "bondwoman" and her children, who represent the legalistic system and the Judaizers and enter the promise by the Spirit.

The Wall of Hostility

"Christ has abolished the law which was a wall of hostility (Ephesians 2:15)"[115]

This is another disastrous quote. It declares the Law to be a wall of hostility. The implication is that the Law, the whole body of Torah, was a wall of hostility against the believer. Furthermore, by the way they lump the Law and the Old Testament together, one could conclude that the Old Testament, the Bible of Jesus and Paul, is hostile toward believers. Actually, that is more or less the conclusion of this author, who slams the Hebrew Scriptures from every angle twisting and distorting Paul's words. Yet, he admits to knowing the explanation here while he discredits it. In any event, Paul was not slamming Torah and calling the Law a wall of hostility. On the contrary, no good believing Jew would ever do that. He is in fact addressing the wall of hostility that existed between Jew and Gentile. Let's take a look at the passage together:

[115] http://www.phildrysdale.com/2012/10/whats-the-role-of-the-law-in-the-new-covenant/

"Therefore remember that formerly you, the Gentiles in the flesh, ***who are called 'Uncircumcision' by the so-called 'Circumcision,'*** *which is performed in the flesh by human hands - remember that you were at that time separate from Christ, excluded from the commonwealth of Israel, and strangers to the covenants of promise, having no hope and without God in the world. But now in Christ Jesus you who formerly were far off have been brought near by the blood of Christ. For He Himself is our peace, who made both groups into one and broke down the barrier of the dividing wall,* ***by abolishing in His flesh the enmity****, (which is)*[116] *the Law of commandments contained in ordinances, so that in Himself He might make the two into one new man, thus establishing peace, and might reconcile them both in one body to God through the cross, by it having put to death the enmity." Eph 2:14-16 (Emphasis Mine)*

The Gentiles were excluded from the covenants and without God in the world. The Jews were set apart by God as his chosen people and, of course, they still are. There was an enmity between them or a "wall of hostility" because of the commandments and ordinances. These are not the 10 Commandments or the moral Torah, which Gentile believers also embrace, but the Kosher laws and ordinances regulating the relationship between Jews and Gentiles, not all of which were Biblical. Many come from Oral Law and Halacha (traditions). Nevertheless, they prevented Jews from relating with Gentiles and created enmity, which was a barrier between the two. The attitude of the Judaizers, whom Paul referred to as the "so-called circumcision," was to recognize this barrier and force the Gentile believers to become circumcised and adhere to these ordinances. However, since Christ has shed His blood as the perfect sacrifice for the sins of all, and both Jewish and Gentile believers are declared righteousness by faith in Him, there is no more enmity. The reason for the wall of division is done away with since Gentiles have been accepted and are no longer considered defiled

[116] The "Which is" is inserted by the translators and is misleading. The NIV does a better job here.

or unclean. They are both reconciled in one body. This is the point of the passage.

Miscellaneous Misleading Quotes

It is easy once one becomes convinced that the Law itself is the problem to find what appears to be damning evidence everywhere. The following statements reflect this kind of bias and show no real study by the author of the passages involved. Examples are the following:

"The law is an unbearable yoke." (Acts 15:10)[117]

This is a conclusion from what Peter said in the famous counsel of Acts 15. What is left out is the context of his remarks, which reveal what he considers an unbearable yoke. Acts chapter 15 begins as follows:

"Some men came down from Judea and began teaching the brethren, ***'Unless you are circumcised according to the custom of Moses, you cannot be saved.'*** *And when Paul and Barnabas had great dissension and debate with them, the brethren determined that Paul and Barnabas and some others of them should go up to Jerusalem to the apostles and elders concerning this issue." Acts 15:1-2 (Emphasis Mine)*

The Legalists told the Gentile believers that they could not be saved unless they became circumcised and followed the Jewish customs. In other words, their faith in Christ was not enough for them to be saved; they also had to become Jews and commit themselves to a works system of righteousness. Paul and Barnabas were sent to Jerusalem from Antioch to the Apostles and elders to look into this matter. It was during this debate that Peter made his remarks.

---

[117] http://www.phildrysdale.com/2012/10/whats-the-role-of-the-law-in-the-new-covenant/

"The apostles and the elders came together to look into this matter. After there had been much debate, Peter stood up and said to them, "Brethren, you know that in the early days God made a choice among you, that by my mouth the Gentiles would hear the word of the gospel and believe. And God, who knows the heart, testified to them giving them the Holy Spirit, just as He also did to us; and He made no distinction between us and them, cleansing their hearts by faith. ***Now therefore why do you put God to the test by placing upon the neck of the disciples a yoke which neither our fathers nor we have been able to bear?*** *But we believe that we are saved through the grace of the Lord Jesus, in the same way as they also are." Acts 15:6-11(Emphasis Mine)*

The context here makes it very clear what Peter was referring to. No good Torah abiding Jew, as Peter was,[118] would refer to the Law of God as an unbearable yoke. The yoke he was referring to was a legalistic system of works righteousness that the nation had become enslaved to. The Gentiles had believed in Christ and were justified by faith just like their Jewish brothers. Therefore, they were not to submit to a system of works righteousness, which Peter and the apostles now understood to be an unbearable yoke.

Paul considered everything the law gained him as "skybalon" which is Greek for "poop". (Philippians 3:4-8)[119]

Not only is this statement false, it is offensive. Paul was not speaking about the Law or anything he got from it. He was talking about his reputation and learning in Judaism, which he considered a result of works and striving in the flesh.

"Beware of the dogs, beware of the evil workers, ***beware of the false circumcision;*** *for we are the true circumcision, who worship in the Spirit of God and glory in Christ Jesus* ***and put no confidence in the flesh,*** *although I myself might have confidence even in the flesh.* ***If***

---

[118] Acts 10:14

[119] http://www.phildrysdale.com/2012/10/whats-the-role-of-the-law-in-the-new-covenant/

***anyone else has a mind to put confidence in the flesh, I far more:** circumcised the eighth day, of the nation of Israel, of the tribe of Benjamin, a Hebrew of Hebrews; as to the Law, a Pharisee; as to zeal, a persecutor of the church; as to the righteousness which is in the Law, found blameless. But whatever things were gain to me, those things I have counted as loss for the sake of Christ. More than that, I count all things to be loss in view of the surpassing value of knowing Christ Jesus my Lord, for whom I have suffered the loss of all things, and count them but rubbish so that I may gain Christ, and may be found in Him, **not having a righteousness of my own derived from the Law**,* (legalism) *but that which is through faith in Christ, the righteousness which comes from God on the basis of faith, that I may know Him and the power of His resurrection and the fellowship of His sufferings, being conformed to His death; in order that I may attain to the resurrection from the dead." Philippians 3:2-11(Emphasis Mine)*

The issue here has nothing to do with the Law but Paul's reputation in Judaism and his credentials as a scholar.[120] He had given his life to a system of works righteousness, which he now considers a work of the flesh. The Judaizers continue to operate in the flesh and put their confidence in their own works. This is the point that Paul is making, that he puts no confidence in fleshly efforts but considers all he had accomplished in Judaism as rubbish compared to knowing Christ. To suggest that all the Law gives one is "skybalon" would be deeply insulting to Paul and all the First Century believers. That would be the equivalent of saying to Christians today, "Everything you get from the Bible is just poop compared to Christ." Need I say anymore?

*"The law is **only** good if used in the right context. (1Timothy 1:8) (see next verse for the context) It was made for the unrighteous but not for the righteous. (1Timothy 1:9-10)"* [121] *(Emphasis Mine)*

---

[120] Galatians 1:14

[121] http://www.phildrysdale.com/2012/10/whats-the-role-of-the-law-in-the-new-covenant/

To say the Law is **only** good if we use it in the right context sounds like what Paul said, but it is not. The author assumes he decides the context. However, the Law is **always** good, holy and righteous regardless of context. What Paul actually said, was, "We know that the Law is good if one uses it lawfully," but the context of his statement is necessary to understand it.

"For some men, straying from these things, have turned aside to fruitless discussion, wanting to be teachers of the Law, even though they do not understand either what they are saying or the matters about which they make confident assertions. But ***we know that the Law is good, if one uses it lawfully****, realizing the fact* ***that law is not made for a righteous person****, but for those who are lawless and rebellious, for the ungodly and sinners, for the unholy and profane, for those who kill their fathers or mothers, for murderers and immoral men and homosexuals and kidnappers and liars and perjurers, and whatever else is contrary to sound teaching, according to the glorious gospel of the blessed God, with which I have been entrusted." 1Tim 1:6-11(Emphasis Mine)*

The difference in these statements may seem to be minuscule but it is actually quite profound. On the one hand, the author of the quote says that the Law is **only** good in a certain context, otherwise it is bad and even dangerous to one's spiritual health. Paul, however, is saying that he and Timothy understand the Law itself is good, but that some people are misusing it or using it unlawfully. In other words, they are abusing it and distorting its true purpose and meaning. He did not say, as he is falsely quoted as saying, that the Law was not made for righteous people but only sinners. What he said was that law (no article) or the moral laws contained in Torah, were made to correct the godless and not the righteous, since they would already keep them. This is similar to what he said in Galatians 3:19 that the Law was given because of transgressions. Obviously, Paul who told Timothy that the man of God was to be trained and equipped in the Scriptures was not saying that the five books of Moses (Torah) were only written for ungodly people. This is an absurd thought that would make the Scriptures unnecessary for those who walk with Christ. What he is saying is that the people who spend all their time in fruitless discussion about matters of the Law, speculating and drawing erroneous conclusions, are using the Law unlawfully. Those who are walking in righteousness do not wish to be constantly debating the moral codes but are more concerned with bearing fruit for Christ.

When Paul says that the laws contained in Torah are only for the unrighteous and ungodly, he also says that the "glorious gospel of the blessed God" which has been entrusted to him concurs with these things. Thus, he is obviously not minimizing the importance of the Law and its condemnation of sinful behavior any more than he is minimizing the gospel and its sound doctrine. He is saying something like what James said in his epistle that these men need to be doers of the word[122] and not trying to make a name for themselves haggling. In other words, if the Ten Commandments are in our hearts then they are automatically part of our lives. We don't need to be constantly preached to about not doing this or that. However, the godless person and the sinner needs to be confronted with the moral code so that he can acknowledge his sin and repent. I believe that is a much fairer and accurate representation of this passage.

Conclusion

There are many more distortions concerning the Law and the writings of Paul being made popular today that need correction, yet there is not enough space to handle them here. Nevertheless, I trust that what has been presented is sufficient to satisfy those seeking a true Biblical perspective. I also trust that it sufficiently illustrates the ungodly attitude toward the Law being proliferated by the Hyper Grace movement and uncovers the roots of this antinomian minefield. I would now like to close this chapter with

---

[122] James 1:22

one thought. At the end of an article, which has been quoted much in this chapter, this statement appears.

"The law is a mirror, but nobody ever uses the mirror to clean themselves. The purpose of a mirror is to show you your dirty face – not to clean it – you need Jesus to clean that dirty face."[123]

After spending a significant amount of time blasting the Law as a curse, the minister of death, the author of slavery, the antithesis of faith, the frustrator of grace, not even worthy to be hung on the wall in Sunday school, he now suggests that it is useful as a mirror to reveal our true spiritual condition. Really? You mean the Law can actually help me. Unbelievable! I am glad that he finally saw the light, but since he has spent so much time condemning the Law of God, his hearers have gotten rid of the mirror already. Now there is nothing to unveil their dirty faces except the lifestyles of the HG teachers. I don't know about you, but I'm holding onto my mirror. It might not be able to clean my face, but if I don't know that my face is dirty, I will probably not present it to Jesus for His cleansing Blood. In fact, not only am I holding onto it, I'm giving it in a prominent place in my life. I intend to keep looking at it often just to be sure, my face is clean and I am walking blamelessly before Him. I am so grateful for His grace that saves me and His blood that cleanses me, but I'm also thankful for the mirror of His commandments and the lamp of His word that make my steps sure.

"But prove yourselves doers of the word, and not merely hearers who delude themselves. For if anyone is a hearer of the word and not a doer, he is like a man who looks at his natural face in a mirror; for once he has looked at himself and gone away, he has immediately forgotten what kind of person he was. But one who looks intently at the perfect law, the law of liberty, and abides by it, not having become a forgetful hearer but an effectual doer, this man will be blessed in what he does." James 1:22-25

---

[123] http://www.phildrysdale.com/2012/10/whats-the-role-of-the-law-in-the-new-covenant/

Chapter 6

A Kinder Gentler God

As a pastor and a healing minister for many years, I am convinced that there is no greater need in the human heart than to know the love of the Father. My wife and I have sat with countless souls, from all occupations, and seen the deep inner pain caused by absentee or abusive dads. Even those who come from loving families are often wounded from a lack of affirmation and acceptance. Consequently, churches and pulpits are filled with people who do not have a personal knowledge of the Fathers love. Indeed, many have difficulty relating to the Father at all because of their experience with or without their father. Besides, all of us tend to project onto God our own view of father. It is not surprising then that the Holy Spirit has been pouring out on the church, for many years now, a fresh revelation of the Father's Heart. Scores of churches have experienced transformation from being works and performance based to becoming rooted and grounded in love.

For me personally, I had known and taught these truths for many years, without a depth of experiential knowledge. My identity was more in what I was doing and accomplishing, or not accomplishing for God, than in the Father Himself. I am happy to say that, though I still struggle from time to time, I am largely at rest in His love and goodness and able to operate from that. Since that transformation took place in my own life, I can say that I have been far more effective and anointed in my ministry. The following passage from Ephesians 3 makes it clear that this is God's design for all of us:

"For this reason I bow my knees before the Father, from whom every family in heaven and on earth derives its name, that He would grant you,

according to the riches of His glory, to be strengthened with power through His Spirit in the inner man, so that Christ may dwell in your hearts through faith; and that you, being rooted and grounded in love, may be able to comprehend with all the saints what is the breadth and length and height and depth, and to know the love of Christ which surpasses knowledge, that you may be filled up to all the fullness of God. Now to Him who is able to do far more abundantly beyond all that we ask or think, according to the power that works within us, to Him be the glory in the church and in Christ Jesus to all generations forever and ever. Amen." Eph 3:14-21

Over the last few years, I have come to see a progression in these verses that begins with our identity in the Father and progresses to a maturity of Christ's love in us to being filled up with His fullness and power. This is the revelation that we see God wanting to bring His church into in these last days, so that we can fulfill His plan out of a place of security and rest in His love.

"Papa God"

"For you have not received a spirit of slavery leading to fear again, but you have received a spirit of adoption as sons by which we cry out, "Abba! Father!" Rom 8:15

I will never forget the first time I heard a young Jewish boy, on the streets of Jerusalem, calling out "Abba" to his father. As a Christian, I had grown up with an understanding that this was the term in Hebrew for "Daddy" and that Paul had exhorted us to relate to God this way. However, it was quite another thing to hear and see it in action on the street. It brought home to me the reality and intimacy of the term. It also underscored the legitimacy of calling God "Daddy" or as some say "Papa," and the importance of being childlike before Him. There is such healthiness in knowing our Heavenly Daddy's heart for us and being able to rest in His loving arms. Yet we must be careful to know Him as He really is and relate to Him based on this knowledge, rather than creating for ourselves the kind of Papa we always wanted.

In every revival of experience and truth there is a tendency to "bounce off the wall" in extremes for a while before coming to a healthy balance. For instance, when folks grow up with overly strict or abusive parents there is tendency for them to be lenient when they become parents themselves out of overreaction. On the other hand, when somebody has been extremely promiscuous before coming to know the Lord, there is a danger of becoming legalistic afterwards out of overreaction. In the same way, there is also the tendency in those who embrace the Father's Heart message, to overcompensate in their view of the Father. They are inclined to major on God's niceness and tenderness at the exclusion of His discipline and correction, which are huge aspects of love and fatherhood.[124]It is true that the Father's love must become our identity and motivator, but we must not neglect or become unhinged from the rest of God's word. God does call some to major on specific messages for a season in order to restore truth; however, it is all the more important that they stay accountable to others and the whole counsel of God.[125] Of course, some will argue with the notion of "balance" seeing it as weakening or compromising the message. There are times when this is true and people who use the idea of balance as a wet blanket. Yet, there is a proper place of balance, which is more an issue of context than a straightjacket. The phrase "out of the box" has become very popular in our time. It has come to be used of "cutting edge ideas", creativity, or even inspiration. However, "out of the box" can be good or bad depending on the box being referred to. I believe it is safe to say that much of what is deemed "out of the box" in revival circles needs to be rescued from private

---

[124] Heb 12:4-11
[125] Acts 20:27

interpretation and put back into the box of sound Biblical exegesis.

The God of the Jews

I once heard a Father Heart speaker give a wonderful testimony that ministered to my soul. I was so impressed with it that I decided to buy the tape series – that's right I said tape series. However, when I got it home and began to listen to the rest of it I was very shocked. In fact, I couldn't believe my ears. The speaker was referring to a song that was popular at the time called "Yahweh." His response was something like this:

"I hate that song Yahweh. I won't sing that song - the God of the Jews."

He went on to talk about the love of the Father but it was clear to me he had made a distinction between the God of the Old Testament and the Father of the Lord Jesus Christ. Of course, it was not that unusual to hear a Christian sort of apologizing for the God of the "Old Testament" as though He was saved when Jesus came, but this was the first time I heard a preacher actually imply that there was a difference between the two. Today however, it is quite common to hear preachers, especially in the Revival Movements, so undermine the Old Testament and its revelation of God that it is hard to imagine this God being the Father of Jesus. Furthermore, it is even harder to imagine that Jesus Himself is this same God, since they consistently paint Him as nicer and gentler. Some have gone so far as to suggest the Jesus of the gospels was a bit stuffy and "under the Law," and that He had to die not only to free us but to free Himself as well. Others thankfully, denounce this and affirm that the teaching of Jesus prior to the Cross is for every Christian, however, they will also try to distance themselves from the Old Testament God whom they see as having a judgmental disposition. Of course, they don't often do it overtly but in a more reverent covert sort of way. For instance, they will say things like "Jesus is perfect theology" or

"Jesus didn't model it" which sounds so Biblical. Who is going to take issue with Jesus as the model? Of course we are to be like Him and walk like Him and do the works that He did and gave us to do and so on. Nevertheless, it is nonsensical to say that Jesus is perfect theology unless we are talking about the full revelation of Jesus in the Bible.

We cannot say that perfect theology is to be determined by what Jesus of Nazareth did and did not do since there is much left out. For example, Jesus did not get married. Therefore, does this mean that it is perfect theology to be single? He did not own a home of His own. Does this mean it is wrong to own a home? Jesus of Nazareth came with a very clear mission and did only what the Father wanted Him to do. When He comes again, He will do things He did not do the first time, like executing vengeance on the wicked and judging the living and the dead. These are also perfect theology, are they not? To say that "Jesus of Nazareth did not model it," is a back door way of saying that the God of Moses was different or not perfect in His theology or character, since He not only healed people but He put diseases on them as punishment.[126] This teaching is pitting Jesus' ministry against the Scriptures and against the apostles who also did things, He did not do, such as; putting blindness on Elymas[127] and death on Ananias and Sapphira.[128] This is also perfect theology because it is the work of the Holy Spirit who evidently didn't get the memo that God never puts sickness on people.

Positively Wrong

This notion that the God of the Old Testament is harsh, vindictive, and different from Jesus of Nazareth, is not a new idea. Indeed, it has been out of the box for a long time. Although the HG teachers and their sympathizers have not said this directly,

---

[126] Num 21:6
[127] Acts 5:1-11
[128] Acts 13:11

if one follows the logic of their arguments about how God sees things, there is no other conclusion to be drawn. Papa God is like a grand old Santa Claus figure without any list of who's naughty or nice. Indeed, all are nice and everything is rosy and positive. I recently read these remarks posted on a social network:

"All of heaven is making war on negativity. They are expecting you to join in. That means that you are responsible for killing negativity stone dead in your life. Take every thought captive, watch what comes out of your mouth and how you look at people. Make war with all forms of negativity in your heart, and then you can be freed to make war on negativity in general."

While it is true that we must speak in agreement with God's word, bless, and curse not, this statement itself is actually at war with heaven. It is not just a call to watch our mouths and speak nothing that grieves the Holy Spirit, but it is "politically correct" propaganda that could have come from any self-help guru. After all, negative is bad and positive is good. We got our Yin and our Yang - positive energy and negative energy. Is this what the gospel has been reduced to? I thought sin was bad and righteousness was good? Where does the Word say, "All of heaven is waging war on negativity" and where does it wage such a war? If these criteria were applied to the Bible itself, it would have to be confiscated by the negativity police. How would Jeremiah, Isaiah, Ezekiel, Jesus or Paul have fared out if this "positive" filter had been applied to their ministry? I do not doubt that this preacher is trying to help people but this teaching is false and deceptive. Those who say that God is waging war on negativity, are making it clear that whatever they deem positive is from God and anyone who disagrees is negative and against God. Thus, they muzzle the opposition and marginalize them as the politicians do. They are actually saying that there is no place for correction or reproof since these things obviously appear negative. Furthermore, they are making it clear that they view God as one who never disciplines, judges, or punishes anyone since that would also have to be negative. Thus, we have the happy God who never gets grieved, never gets upset or angry at anything – the kinder gentler God of the sterilized New Testament. However, the HG God does get angry with the "religious" who disagree with the "positive only" message, and when addressing them, negativity is not only condoned, but often encouraged.

Return of the Demiurge

In the 2nd Century, Marcion of Sinope was a Christian leader who actually taught that the God of the Old Testament was cruel and vindictive and not the Father of our Lord Jesus Christ. He called him the Demiurge, who although he was the creator, was a jealous tribal deity whose law was one of legalistic justice - the god of the Jews. The Father of our Lord Jesus, on the other hand, was a good and compassionate God of love and mercy.

Though Marcion was not a classic Gnostic, he had much in common with Gnostic teaching. He formed his own Canon of Scripture, which included an edited version of the gospel of Luke and ten of Paul's epistles, whom Marcion believed to be the correct interpreter of Jesus' teachings. It wasn't that Marcion, believed the Old Testament was false, but that since it was about a lesser legalistic, vindictive god, it was not to be seen as authoritative. The other Jewish apostles, of course, did not represent the God of grace properly and thus were discarded. Sound familiar? I have no doubt that if Marcion were alive today he would be very happy in the Revival Movement and would be well known and loved. As it turns out, he was excommunicated by the church, and led a strong vibrant heretical movement that survived and rivaled the Christian Church for centuries.

Though the Hyper Grace movement does not embrace the teachings of Marcion, their attitude toward Scripture and the revelation of God in the Old Testament, is virtually identical.

Sure, they don't claim that there are two gods, but their teachings lead down the same path. They change the nature of God with new assertions and doctrines opposed to the revelation of God in Scripture, and any verses that challenge are relegated to a false interpretation by the legalists. By cataloguing the Old Testament and even the teachings of Jesus as belonging to a more primitive, less enlightened, religious time, they skirt their understanding and application. Those left that contain law or negativity apply to the unsaved. Thus, they achieve the same result as Marcion as they replace the God of the Bible with a lesser deity of their own creation who is totally benign and manageable. Does this seem a bit farfetched? Do you think I am exaggerating? I wish I were! Perhaps I am speaking more out of a place of foresight, having connected the dots, but there is ample evidence already that this movement is giving the God of the Bible a serious makeover.

God Not in Control

One of the latest rants becoming extremely popular in the church is the idea that God is not in control of things. Can you believe it? Almighty God, who made the heavens and the earth and all that in in them, is not in control of everything. If this were not so dangerous, it would be laughable, but here are some quotes from some of the most popular Charismatic and Revivalist teachers.

"God is not in control because he put us in charge of the earth. Who is in charge of the earth? We are! ...If God had retained control of the earth as many believe, then when Adam began lifting the forbidden fruit towards his mouth, God would have intervened and slapped it from his hand."

"One of the biggest areas of confusion we have within the church is concerning the sovereignty of God. We know that God is all-powerful. We know that he is in charge of everything. But with that, we make a mistake of thinking that he is in control of everything. There's a difference between being in charge and being in control. If you believe that he is

control of everything, then you have to believe that Hitler was within his will - that he was going to work it for his purposes."

After nearly forty years in Christian ministry, it is unimaginable that mainstream Christian leaders would teach such foolishness. Nevertheless, they are, and the motive appears to be a remake of God to mollycoddle the masses and give credence to their dominion agenda. After all, who has not been asked why a loving God allows bad things to happen? Indeed, every Christian will face this question, which sounds so reasonable but is actually an affront on the character of God by a man-centered, humanistic, rebellious human race that sees itself as the center of the universe. It is the clay telling the potter that his creation is flawed and His character untrustworthy because the process and design is not to his liking. However, the ancient Hebrews, who gave us the revelation of God contained in the Bible, never felt the need to apologize for His actions or sanitize His judgments. The idea of a god not in control with his hands tied behind his back was reserved for the likes of Dagon and Baal and not the Creator of the Universe. They could never have conceived that the existence of evil and atrocity was proof that the Holy One had surrendered his personal involvement and supervision of the planet. Their worldview could never allow this. There was no question as to why evil and atrocity existed. God created everything. Evil existed so that his creatures would have a free choice - and of course, they chose evil. This is a nursery school lesson. How can we choose to love God and follow His way of love if there is no other choice? There is no heavy mystery here. The mystery lies in the personhood of God and His eternal existence and not in the proliferation of sin and death on the planet. This is clearly explained in the pages of Scripture. Let us take a moment then to reiterate what the Bible teaches on this matter for those who are unfamiliar or have been confused by current teaching.

"Therefore, just as through one man sin entered into the world, and death through sin, and so death spread to all men, because all sinned..." Rom 5:12

According to Paul (and he should know), the sin of Adam is the reason that death, sickness and judgment entered the world. It is a straightforward statement. Humanity aligned itself with satan and rebelled against God and has been doing so ever since. Thus, the sin of man is the source of all the trouble and suffering on the planet not only for humans but also for all creation.[129] Sin entered the world and corruption through sin. Corruption is death in progress and sickness is a result of corruption. Bad things happen because of corruption and death in creation, such as storms, devastating floods, sickness, etc. Evil things happen because of the continued sin and wickedness of humanity. If humanity were destroyed, evil and injustice would cease. In fact, because of the evil intent of humanity, God destroyed the world millennia ago preserving only Noah and his family.

"Then the LORD saw that the wickedness of man was great on the earth, and that every intent of the thoughts of his heart was only evil continually. The LORD was sorry that He had made man on the earth, and He was grieved in His heart. The LORD said, 'I will blot out man whom I have created from the face of the land, from man to animals to creeping things and to birds of the sky; for I am sorry that I have made them.' But Noah found favor in the eyes of the LORD." Gen 6:5-8

Though liberal "scholars" find it hard to accept a literal ark and a literal flood, a literal account is given to us by Moses and confirmed by Jesus Himself.[130] This is hardly evidence of a creator who has given up control and dominion of the planet. Neither is it evidence that satan has jurisdiction for the earth is the Lord's and

---

[129] Rom 20-21

[130] Mt 24:38-39

all it contains.[131]Nevertheless, we are being told that if God were really in control, there would be no darkness and human suffering. He is "in charge" they say, but not in control, "otherwise we have to believe that Hitler was within His will." It sounds so convincing, right? After all, how could a loving God who is in control allow that? Our Heavenly Papa is too nice to ever will the massacre of people. Really? Then somebody needs to explain what happened to the ancient Canaanites or the residents of Sodom and Gomorrah. Who was the one who made the sun stand still so that Joshua could slaughter the Amorites?[132] The one in charge or the one in control? Who told the nation of Israel that He would scatter them to the nations and draw out a sword after them?[133] Who promised to send hunters after Israel to hunt them from the clefts of the rocks?[134] The God who is in control or only in charge? Of course, they will say, "That's the Old Testament." God was angry then but since Christ died, He no longer gets like that. "Jesus didn't model it," and "Jesus is perfect theology." But wasn't it Jesus who told His generation of Jews that the wrath of God, for all the righteous blood shed from Abel to Zechariah, would be poured out on them even after the cross?[135] Did He sanction that or was He merely reporting? Who ordered the destruction of Jerusalem and the slaughter of over one million people, men, women and children within its walls?[136] Did Jesus not also prophesy the wrath to come at the end of this age and a time of tribulation so intense that unless it had been cut short, out of nearly eight billion people, no life would be saved? Who raised up Pharaoh? Who slaughtered all the first born of Israel and forced them into hard labor? And who was it that hardened His heart?[137] Surely, I can go on and on. One has to wonder do these preachers actually read the Bible anymore. Have they forgotten

---

[131] Ps 24:1
[132] Joshua 10
[133] Jer 9:16
[134] Jer 16:16
[135] Mt 23:34-36, Luke 21:20-22
[136] Mt 23:34-39
[137] Ex 7:3, Rom 9:17

whom it is they are representing? Just consider the following passages that testify of God's sovereignty and control over all things:

***"The Lord reigns**, let the peoples tremble; He is enthroned above the cherubim, let the earth shake!" Ps99:1 (Emphasis Mine)*

*"The LORD has established His throne in the heavens, and **His sovereignty rules over all**." Ps 103:19 (Emphasis Mine)*

The Lord is not a figurehead like Queen Elizabeth. When it says He rules and reigns over all, it means He actually has control of everything.

*"The Lord **kills and makes alive**; He brings down to Sheol and raises up." 1Sam 2:6 (Emphasis Mine)*

*"That men may know from the rising to the setting of the sun that there is no one besides Me. I am the LORD, and there is no other, the One forming light and **creating darkness**, causing well-being and **creating calamity**; I am the LORD who does **all these**." Is45:6-7 (Emphasis Mine)*

Does God create calamity? That is what it says. He created light and darkness and He also created the devil and allows him to continue his work of tempting mankind. He even allowed him to test Jesus. Does God create all calamity? No! We do quite a good job on our own. Yet He is in control of all and can and does create calamity sometimes to exercise His justice and control. Consider what happened to Herod when he stepped over the line (Acts 12:20-25). Please remember that this was after the cross, during the ministry of the church, when this stuff was not supposed to happen anymore. Also even within the church, God exercised control and judgment on Ananias and Sapphira. Was this a calamity? It was for them. Certainly if you had been there and they were your friends or family members, you would have thought so too. The explanation about this, being an exception and not the rule, might have been hard to swallow. This does not mean however, that God is the author of evil, since evil is rebellion against His will or desire. Neither does it mean that sickness or premature death are His will but it does mean that He allows and even causes them sometimes.

There is a difference between what we call the Perfect Will of God (His desire) and the Permissive Will of God (what He allows). God does not desire or want bad things to happen to people but they are a result of the fall. God can and does intervene directly or through a believer sometimes, but mostly He does not. However, when people turn to Him He works it out for their good – yet, we do reap what we sow.[138] The truth is that the majority of people have to go through difficulties in order to turn to God. And even for Christians, trials are sometimes necessary for the testing and proving of our faith.[139] Therefore, those who wish to make God's actions always positive according to their viewpoint have a problem with His justice, His judgments and even His methods in reaching the lost or refining our faith.

"The Most High is ruler over the realm of mankind and bestows it on whomever He wishes." Dan 4:32

"Are not five sparrows sold for two cents? Yet not one of them is forgotten before God. Indeed, the very hairs of your head are all numbered. Do not fear; you are more valuable than many sparrows." Luke 12:6-7

"And we know that God causes all things to work together for good to those who love God, to those who are called according to His purpose." Rom 8:28

---

[138] Gal 6:8

[139] James 1:2-3, 1Pet 1:6-9

"For God ***has shut up all in disobedience*** *so that He may show mercy to all. Oh, the depth of the riches both of the wisdom and knowledge of God! How unsearchable are His judgments and unfathomable His ways! For WHO HAS KNOWN THE MIND OF THE LORD, OR WHO BECAME HIS COUNSELOR? Or WHO HAS FIRST GIVEN TO HIM THAT IT MIGHT BE PAID BACK TO HIM AGAIN?* ***For from Him and through Him and to Him are all things****. To Him be the glory forever. Amen." Rom 11:32-36 (Emphasis Mine)*

"In Him also we have obtained an inheritance, having been predestined according to His purpose who works ***all things*** *after the counsel of His will." Eph 1:11 (Emphasis Mine)*

"For it is God who is at work in you, both to will and to work for His good pleasure." Phil 2:13

There is perhaps nothing more absurd being spoken today than the notion that God is not in control. Has the Almighty lost control over His creation? If so, we are doomed. There is no comfort in adding that He is in charge. How can that be? To be in charge is to be in control. When one gives up control one gives up charge as well. Has God lost the ability to intervene in the affairs of men anytime He wants to? If so, He is not sovereign or almighty. Moreover, to say that He is in charge but not in control does not make Him more benevolent. In fact, it demeans His character by suggesting that He is not willing or powerful enough to do anything about evil and human suffering. On the one hand, He is willing to just let the world limp along, and on the other, it raises the possibility that evil may actually win. Of course, those who teach this believe that He has relinquished control and dominion to the church and it is now up to us to change things. The battle is no longer His but ours. (He just watches, I guess.) We are responsible to bring in the kingdom and enforce His rule. If sickness is not healed, nations are not won, and the earth is not subject to Christ, it is our fault. However, that is even more frightening. If the future of the earth is in the hands of the church, we are of all men to be pitied. As the saying goes, "Been there, done that." Dear friend, as much as I love the church, and as much as I am committed to the kingdom, it is utter foolishness to suggest that the church is the hope of the world. Christ has given the church authority but He has not, and never will, relinquish His control to human beings.

It is astonishing how those who believe in a caring God who is involved in every area of our lives, could have tied His hands behind His back so He is unable to do anything unless we beg and plead. It is true that we must walk in faith but it is not true that God has left it all up to us. Friends, I am not in any way diminishing the role of prayer and intercession, but it is not to give God permission or ability to act. God does not need our permission or intercession to do anything. He gave us the privilege of being fellow workers with Him, and chooses to work through us, but that does not mean He is dependent on us. On the contrary, He is totally in charge and firmly in control. We have been commissioned and given authority and power to act in His Name, but we have not been given control. Perish the thought! The Holy Spirit is in control. He is Lord in the church. Lord means boss, which means control. This is Christianity 101. Read the book of Acts and tell me who was in control. Study history for the last two thousand years and tell me if the Lord has relinquished control to the church. Better still, study church history and tell me if there would even be a church or a gospel had the Holy Spirit not intervened repeatedly and exercised His control. Surely, those who have come out of revival know this - or have they become so arrogant to think it is now all about them and their new understanding and "apostolic anointing?" Heaven help them if it is!

The Lord is our Healer

Another reason that this notion of God being in charge but not in control was invented was to explain why Christians get sick and sometimes die and why the people we pray for are not always healed. There is no doubt that this is difficult to understand, and that the church is lacking in the area of healing. However, as we are becoming more in sync with the Holy Spirit, and what He is doing, we are seeing a great many more healings and miracles. It is true that in order to see the sick healed we must believe and know that healing is God's will for them. It is definitely the children's bread[140] and part of the gospel message.[141] Sickness is not something God wants for anybody. It is definitely not His will for His children. This is clearly demonstrated for us in the Bible under the Old Covenant and the New. The Lord is our healer.[142] It is His desire for us to lay hands on the sick and see them recover. Disease is definitely not something that glorifies Him in any way. Nevertheless, there are exceptions to the norm and other factors that can hinder healing. Jesus Himself was limited by the lack of faith in Nazareth. And even Paul, who was mighty in miracles, had to watch his friend and fellow apostle Epaphroditus nearly die, and admitted that if God had not "had mercy" on him he would have had "sorrow upon sorrow."[143] Therefore, it is clear that Paul did not consider himself the healer or think that it would have been his fault had Epaphroditus died. Thus, there is a place in healing where we must defer to the mercy and sovereignty of God without using it as an excuse for unbelief. The Lord is still The Healer and even when we heal the sick or do miracles, we do it in His Name and with His authority and not our own. Furthermore, healings and miracles in themselves are not proof that our teaching is right or that our ministry is validated.[144] Why then, is it necessary to declare that God is not in control and we are, and that if someone is not healed it is our fault? Surely, this demeans the Almighty and is a recipe for human effort and striving - a focus on man rather than God. Furthermore, while

---

[140] Mt 15:26
[141] Luke 4:18-19
[142] Ex 15:26
[143] Phil 2:25-27
[144] Mt 7:21-23

those who put all the onus on the church to heal the sick are purported to be seeing great miracles, there are also many walking away from their meetings unhealed. How then is God spared the blame when folks are not healed? Indeed, rather than making God seem more kind and benevolent, it makes Him seem more distant, less caring, unpredictable and perhaps cruel, since despite the minister's best effort, incredible faith and "apostolic anointing," people are still dying. Why not just operate in faith and leave the things we do not understand in God's hands. How does that limit God? However, they will argue that it does since we are aware that some will not be healed and we have allowed for that in our theology. I understand the argument, but even if I believe that God always heals and it's up to me to get them healed, I am still aware that not everyone is getting healed so the so called "door to doubt" is still open. Not only that, there are other doors open as well. For instance, say ten people come to me for healing of cancer. I pray and nine are healed but the other one dies. Now I did everything right, and had loads of faith and trust for all nine but I failed the one person who died. And not only that, God let me fail with that one person and was unable for some reason to back me up. Thus, I healed the nine but failed to heal the one and nobody knows why. So now, I have become the healer rather than Jesus. It is all up to me. I have now lowered God and exalted man. Make no mistake about it, this teaching is false and will lead to ruin.

Another conclusion being advanced with the "God is not in control" teaching, is the notion that Jesus walked the earth as a man and not God. He laid aside His Godhood and was powerless to act on His own, they say. In other words, Jesus did everything He did as a mere man being led by the Spirit. If He did something as God then it would mean that we could not follow in His steps. Therefore, He worked powerful healings and miracles as a mere man anointed by the Holy Spirit. However, that argument is false. Jesus did not cease to be God when He became Jesus of Nazareth.

He was not powerless as these preachers claim. What He actually said was that He could do nothing of Himself or of His own initiative.[145] He was perfectly capable of turning the stones to bread or jumping off the Temple and gliding to the ground if He wanted too - things, which were not the Father's will for Him. Otherwise, this would not have been a real temptation, as it had to be. Furthermore, to say that Jesus was merely a man when He walked the earth is demeaning to who He was and is actually contradictory to His message. He was and is the Son of God – God Himself incarnate. He was the Messiah, the Anointed One, the Way, the Truth and The Life. No one, including Moses, was equal in stature with Him or greater in the things they did or in the way they spoke. He was and is the one and only unique Son of God – the I Am and the Alpha and Omega. This is the whole point of the gospel. He was always one with the Father and when He became a man, He continued to be one with the Father. Though He could have operated outside of the Father's authority and was tempted to do so, He chose not to. He told His disciples that if they had seen Him, they had seen the Father.

It is true that Christ was exalted in His flesh after the resurrection, but this did not change who He was before. He was the sinless Son of God who became a sin offering on the cross and in His flesh paid the penalty for our sins. He did not become sinful or blemished by this act needing to be born again, as some are now asserting,[146] but He was always sinless and perfect. John himself declared of Jesus of Nazareth:

---

[145] John 5:19, John 8:28

[146] Many in the Charismatic and Revival Movements are now claiming that Jesus became sin and died spiritually and had to be born again. They distort Paul's words in 1Cor 5:21 to suggest that Jesus actually became sin itself or sinful on the cross and died spiritually. Paul however, was referring to Jesus as the sin offering who took the sins on His body and carried them away as the Yom Kippur scapegoat. The sins were transferred to Him so to speak and He took them away. Jesus was both Yom Kippur goats, the one who was offered for the sins of the people and the one who carried them away. He did not cease to be holy and sinless and did not die spiritually and need regeneration in His Spirit. He remained the perfect Son of God throughout the suffering of the cross. Peter affirms this in 1Pet 2:24 when He declares that He bore our sins **on His body** on the cross so that we might die to sin and live to righteousness.

"And the Word became flesh, and dwelt among us, and we saw His glory, glory as of the only begotten from the Father, full of grace and truth." John 1:14

It is true that we are called to walk as He walked and go out in His name, and yes, even do greater works. However, this is only possible because Jesus sent us another like Himself, the Holy Spirit, who is also God. As we receive Christ's authority and obey the Spirit, we can certainly accomplish much, but that does not make us Christ or Jesus of Nazareth a mere anointed man. Whatever we do, we can only do it in His name and with His authority and power. We are not little gods walking around. It is not necessary to lower Christ and exalt man in order to do the works of the kingdom. Neither is it necessary to make up new doctrines about His sovereignty and control in order to operate in His anointing and power.

Yesterday, Today and Forever

When the author of Hebrews declared that Jesus Christ is the same yesterday, today and forever,[147] he was not getting his information from the New Testament, since it did not exist at the time. Neither was he concluding this merely from his own personal knowledge and experience. He was surely basing his emphatic statement on the revelation of God contained in the so-called "Old Testament" – the Bible of the early church. He likely had passages like this in mind:

*"'**I am the first and I am the last, and there is no God besides Me.** Who is like Me? Let him proclaim and declare it; yes, let him recount it to Me in order, from the time that I established the ancient nation. And let them declare to them the things that are coming and the events that are going to take place. Do not tremble and do not be afraid; have I not long since announced it to you and declared it? And you are My witnesses.*

[147] Heb 13:8

Is there any God besides Me, or is there any other Rock? I know of none.'" *Is 44:7-8 (Emphasis Mine)*

"For I, the LORD, do not change; *therefore you, O sons of Jacob, are not consumed." Mal 3:6 (Emphasis Mine)*

The early church spread the gospel throughout the world. They were mighty in power and the Scriptures. They did not see any disconnect between the Bible (OT) and the gospel message. Neither did they see any difference between the God of Moses and the God and Father of Our Lord Jesus Christ. They were able to open up passage after passage and reveal the Lord Jesus and never needed to say, "Oh that's the Old Testament." They were perfectly comfortable with the love of God and the wrath of God. They would have been sickened by the thought of believers apologizing for the harshness of the God of Israel, or the judgments that befell the Ancient Canaanites and the Israelites themselves. However, the church today could scarcely find a connection between the Father of Love they preach and the Yahweh of Moses. They can perhaps open Is 53 or Psalm 22 and show the love of Jesus and His sufferings on the cross. However, would they be able to turn to the story of the Exodus and reveal the Father Heart of God? Could they explain that the Lord who showed His glory to Moses is the same Father who hugged and kissed the prodigal? If not, why not? The apostles certainly did and so did Jesus Himself.

It is time for the modern church, Charismatics, Pentecostals and Evangelicals alike, to repent for its constant berating of the Old Testament and separating Jesus of Nazareth from His God chosen Jewish traditions and Biblical culture. It is time to stop speaking or implying that there is a New Testament God who is different from the Old Testament One, and a modern Hippy-Like Jesus with flowers in His hair. Wouldn't it be better to get rid of this "Old Testament, New Testament" lingo altogether and refer to the entire Bible with the love and respect due the inerrant Word of God. It is time to get to know the God of the Bible as Christ and the Scriptures reveal Him, and stop trying to make Him compatible with a rebellious world that rejects accountability. Therefore, I would like to end this chapter with a challenge to all believers to be acquainted with the God of our Lord Jesus Christ, who revealed His sevenfold character to Moses, and begin to use this passage in your teaching without leaving out His justice.

"So he cut out two stone tablets like the former ones, and Moses rose up early in the morning and went up to Mount Sinai, as the LORD had commanded him, and he took two stone tablets in his hand. The LORD descended in the cloud and stood there with him as he called upon the name of the LORD. Then the LORD passed by in front of him and proclaimed, 'The LORD, the LORD God, ***compassionate and gracious, slow to anger, and abounding in lovingkindness and truth; who keeps lovingkindness for thousands, who forgives iniquity, transgression and sin; yet He will by no means leave the guilty unpunished, visiting the iniquity of fathers on the children and on the grandchildren to the third and fourth generations.*** *' Moses made haste to bow low toward the earth and worship." Exodus 34:4-8 (Emphasis Mine)*

Seven is a very important number in the Bible. It is the number of completion. The above seven characteristics reveal what the unchanging God is like. They are as follows:

Compassionate
Gracious
Slow to Anger
Abounding in Loving-kindness
Abounding in Truth
Forgives Iniquity and Sin
He will not leave the Guilty Unpunished

From this passage, we can clearly see that our God is a God of love and compassion. Six of the above-mentioned characteristics are about loving-kindness, grace and long-suffering. Only one is about justice and punishment, yet it is all that the modern church knows of the God of Moses. However, without justice, there is no love. Those who exclude the justice and wrath of God from their message are giving their hearers a skewed and false representation of Christ. Jesus Christ is the exact representation of the Father[148] and though He took the wrath of God for all our sins, His character has not changed. He still gets angry and He still judges.[149] The cross not only reminds us of His love, it also reminds us of His wrath. For those who have received Him, embracing the cross and letting it do its work in them, there is joy unspeakable and full of glory. But for those who do not obey Him there is only wrath and indignation.[150] Those who proclaim a "Happy Gospel" and present a God who never gets angry or upset with anything anymore, are misrepresenting Christ and are giving false hope to a world that is already under His judgment.[151] Jesus is coming again soon and when He comes, He will judge the living and the dead. Let us therefore present them with the message of God's grace and love, being mindful of what it cost Him, and making no apologies for His justice and judgments. Let us also remember that the God of the Bible is the one who is perfect, and human beings are the ones needing a makeover.

[148] Heb 1:3

[149] Luke 12:46, Rev 2:5, 16, 19:11-16

[150] Rom 2:8

[151] Rom 1:18

Chapter 7

The New Subjective Bible

Recently there has been a national discussion regarding the comments of a certain reality show star, who, while referring to deviant behavior, quoted from 1Cor 6:9. Though many of the talking heads defended the TV personality, the majority were shocked by his use of the Bible. After all, he was not a Theologian or a scholar and unqualified in their minds to interpret the Biblical passage, even though it needs no interpretation. One well-known talking head, who has written a bestselling book on the life of Jesus, commented that the "Old Testament was hard on homosexuality." I nearly fell of my chair. It was one of those rare moments when my TV almost became a victim. "The Old Testament is hard on homosexuality." Really? By this statement this renowned author, who claims to have more knowledge of the crucifixion than John the apostle, who was there, revealed his absolute ignorance of Scripture. Apparently he has no knowledge of 1Cor 6, Rom 1:26-27, Gal 5 or 1Tim 1:10. Either that or he has found some way to bag these verses and escape their obvious meaning. Of course, I shouldn't be surprised since this individual, though it is clear he believes in Christ, does not know Him and does not see the Bible as authoritative. He has made it clear in the past that it is not to be taken literally and that much of it (the Old Testament of course) is merely a collection of stories. Yet, it is hard to understand the intellectual dishonesty that people sometimes display when it comes to passages of Scripture they want to ignore.

It is no great shock of course, that the world doesn't want to believe the Bible. Neither is it surprising that it should come under attack by folks who claim to belong to Christ. False teachers have questioned its authority and accuracy from the First

Century on. Nevertheless, what is most troubling today is the subtlety, the success and the source of the assaults, and the Biblical illiteracy of this generation. It appears it has been set up for a wave of deception like no other. We are living at the end of the age and the Bible itself warned us that this would happen. Jesus told us that the devil would do everything in his power to deceive the people of God. And history has taught us that the greatest and most effective strategy in all warfare is the one that goes undetected – the one that comes from inside the camp. Therefore, it is clear from the level of undermining and distorting of Scripture that is taking place today, not just on the outskirts or the liberal fringes, but in what is accepted as the mainstream of Christianity, that satan's last great antichrist assault has already begun. Therefore, it is fitting in the last chapter of this volume, to examine the roots of this infiltration and the weak defenses that allow it access. We must take a hard look at what the integrity of Scripture means to us, and be willing to confront whatever attitudes and lapses of judgment have caused so many pastors and leaders to be deaf to its detractors.

Doctrine Divides

Perhaps you have heard that the word of God is a sword, but have you understood that your Bible is also a canon? By a canon, I don't mean a great big gun shooting bowling balls. The word KANON in Greek means, "measuring stick." The Bible is a collection of books that include the Hebrew Scriptures and the New Testament writings of the early church. They were put together and accepted as the Canon or measuring stick by the church in the 2nd Century largely in response to Heresies and attacks on the Scriptures by the likes of Marcion. The Bible is the inerrant, authoritative word of God and has been accepted and honored as such by Christians for two thousand years. It has also been attacked vehemently throughout the ages, yet never more than at the present time. Most "Mainline" and "Liberal Churches" and the so-called "Emerging Church" no longer consider it authoritative and sadly, many in the Charismatic and Revival Movement frequently undermine it as well. Most don't do it out of disrespect and unbelief in the Bible, but because they have succumbed to the notion that reliance on its truth alone is old fashioned, "religious," and insensitive in a so-called "postmodern" culture. They often say things like, "There are so many divisions over Bible doctrine and stuff, who knows who is right?" "Why does it matter so much?" "Why don't we just follow the Spirit and do what we hear Him saying?" "Isn't that the point of the Bible anyway?" These are arguments commonly presented as wisdom by a flippant, celebrity-crazed Christian culture, yet they are fallacious and about as dangerous as shooting oneself in the head. And they don't just come from young ministry school students who have never actually read the Bible, but from a host of pastors and leaders who consider Biblical Scholarship and Theology about as necessary as stained glass windows. Nevertheless, we are now paying the price for this disdain of doctrine. The modern church is reeling from its lack of adherence to the Biblical plumb line. Having ignored the lessons of history she is now dangling over a pit of apostasy. This is the shaking of God. This is the judgment that we are told will begin with His house.[152] Just like the culture that refuses to be accountable to the revelation of God's Word, the church is dangerously close to the same precipice. Dear friends it is time to wake up. The Bible is not just a book. It is the Word of the Living God. It is not an add-on or a sermon source. Without its objective truth, there is nothing reliable. Indeed, if the Scriptures are not totally sure and trustworthy, then neither is our relationship with God. We cannot base anything we are doing on personal experience and revelation of the Spirit. We are to be filled with and led by the Spirit, but without the measuring stick of Scripture, we are unable to know where we are going and who is guiding us. That is why God gave us the Scriptures. His word is

---

[152] 1Pet 4:17

a lamp to our feet and a light to our path.[153] Listen for a minute to what the Bible says about itself:

"Jesus said to them, "Is this not the reason you are mistaken, that you do not understand ***the Scriptures or the power of God****?" Mark 12:24 (Emphasis Mine)*

*"...****The Scripture cannot be broken****..." John 10:35*

"For truly I say to you, until heaven and earth pass away, not the smallest letter or stroke shall pass from the Law until all is accomplished. Whoever then annuls one of the least of these commandments, and teaches others to do the same, shall be called least in the kingdom of heaven; but whoever keeps and teaches them, he shall be called great in the kingdom of heaven." Mt 5:18-19

Make no mistake about it; Jesus did not consider the Scriptures to have any flaws or mistakes. He presented them as an immovable and unbreakable measuring rod and plumb line that is to be loved and adhered to by all His followers.

"Paul, a bond-servant of Christ Jesus, called as an apostle, set apart for the gospel of God, which He promised beforehand through His prophets in the ***Holy Scriptures****..." Rom 1:1 (Emphasis Mine)*

"...and that from childhood you have known ***the sacred writings*** *which are able to give you the wisdom that leads to salvation through faith which is in Christ Jesus." 2Tim 3:15 (Emphasis Mine)*

Notice how Paul affirms that the Book itself is holy.

"For ***whatever was written*** *in earlier times was written for our instruction, so that through perseverance and the* ***encouragement of the Scriptures we might have hope****." Rom 15:4 (Emphasis Mine)*

---

[153] Ps 119:105

*"**All Scripture** is inspired by God and profitable for teaching, for reproof, for correction, for training in righteousness so that the man of God may be adequate, equipped for every good work." 2Tim 3:16-17 (Emphasis Mine)*

All Scripture is God-breathed. It does not need to be breathed upon by the Spirit or anointed again as some assert. The Holy Spirit is already in it and on it. Notice Paul said that "All Scripture" was not only God's word, but that it was necessary for the training and equipping of every man and woman of God.

*"But know this first of all, that **no prophecy of Scripture is a matter of one's own interpretation**..." 2Pet 1:20 (Emphasis Mine)*

The Bible has one interpretation that was intended by the author under the direction of the Holy Spirit. That is not to say that principles cannot be taken and applied to other situations and events, but one does not have the right to offer a private interpretation or understanding. If pastors and leaders took this seriously, there would be a lot more dialogue and accountability in Bible teaching, and we would not be afraid to have our views challenged for fear we should be in error. It was this respect and submission to the Scriptures that caused Paul, who had received His message and commissioning directly from Christ, to discuss his teaching with the apostles in Jerusalem for fear that he might be in error.[154]

*"...just as also our beloved brother Paul, according to the wisdom given him, wrote to you, as also in all his letters, speaking in them of these things, in which are some things hard to understand, **which the untaught and unstable distort, as they do also the rest of the Scriptures, to their own destruction.**" 2Pet 3:15-16 (Emphasis Mine)*

[154] Gal 2:2

Peter made it clear why people distort the Scriptures. He gave two reasons, ignorance and instability of character. He also made it clear that destruction would befall those who did the distorting.

"Beloved, while I was making every effort to write you about our common salvation, I felt the necessity to write to you appealing that you ***contend earnestly for the faith which was once for all handed down to the saints.*** *For certain persons have crept in unnoticed, those who were long beforehand marked out for this condemnation, ungodly persons who turn the grace of our God into licentiousness and deny our only Master and Lord, Jesus Christ." Jude 1:3-4 (Emphasis Mine)*

Jude warns us about those who turn the grace of God into licentiousness. There are to be sure, HG teachers who do not promote licentiousness, yet the HG message will, in time, lead in this direction and eventually to denying the Master Himself. However, we must all carefully heed the warning and contend for the faith that has been delivered to us. This is not contending for one's personal revelation or ministry emphasis, but for the truth and integrity of the Scriptures, since that is what has been "handed down" to us. Though this is not a call to be contentious or to operate in a critical spirit, it is clear that we should not give a pass to people who skate dangerously close to the edge, regardless of the size of their ministries or their relationship to us. Though the Scriptures are true regardless, and will outlast all of us, we must be prepared to defend the integrity and authority of the Bible against every challenge, no matter where it comes from. This attitude, together with the love of God for His people, will protect, unify and equip the church. Sound doctrine does not divide, and if it does then it is a necessary division.[155]

Those who say their concern for unity requires them to be lax in their demand for Biblical accuracy are actually causing disunity by their negligence and unwitting approval of Biblical distortions.

[155] Mt 10:34, 1Cor 11:19

There is not much point to all being in the same boat should the voyage be that of the Titanic. Sound doctrine does not cause division among those who love the truth. Rather, it is those whose hearts are not right, who distort the Word and disobey its teaching, that cause division among believers. Thus giving them license to do so will not bring godly unity. It is time, therefore, for all pastors and teachers who care about their spiritual future and that of their churches, to stop making statements and giving off attitudes that demean the authority and integrity of Scripture. The Bible is Holy and should be treated as such. Those who love Christ and are filled with the Holy Spirit love the Scriptures also. Failure to love and study the Scriptures, and hold fast to **all** the counsel of God, always leads to deception and darkness. Let us now take a moment to look at some of the common attitudes and actions that may be well-meaning, but are helping to lead the modern church away from the safety of Scripture into the murky waters of subjectivity.

Holy Spirit or Holy Book?

Throughout the Twentieth Century, there has been a great outpouring of the Holy Spirit on the church. Several major revivals restored to believers the reality of the gift of the Holy Spirit. For approximately twenty years now, we have been in a fresh wave with the tangible presence of God sweeping through our churches. The Lord is preparing His Bride for the end of the age and His soon return. Yet, there are many, even among the "Spirit-filled" churches that have been unwilling to embrace this Revival. Furthermore, the attacks that have come from those who claim to be the defenders of the faith have been ferocious and cruel. Without examining the fruit and listening to the testimonies, they have been willing to brand almost everyone who has been touched by it as a heretic. These same people who cry out for revival are totally unwilling to listen and even check the history of past revivals that they supposedly revere, to see that the same manifestations have been present in all moves of God since the book of Acts. And while they claim to be the ones who are true to Scripture, they seem to have no place in their theology for the Holy Spirit and His effects on people which are well documented in the same. Nevertheless, it seems that many of our dear friends who were so powerfully affected by this move of God, have overreacted and begun to pit the Holy Spirit Himself against the very Word that He spoke. However, sound doctrine does not come from overreactions, but from the objective teaching of the Bible kept in its correct context and original meaning. There is no tension between the Holy Spirit and the Scriptures and to create it is to dishonor both. However, lacking wisdom and going too far,[156] some of our dear friends are doing just that. Consider the following statements by well-known and well-loved ministries:

"The goal of the Bible is not to know the Bible - the goal is to know the author. The Bible is written in such a way that you need the Spirit of God to know how to apply the Word of God."

While I understand the point being made here, the statement suggests that knowing the Bible is secondary to personal experience. This may be technically true, but it is not sound, since it tends to plant in the mind of the hearer the idea that subjective thoughts and feelings are more valid and spiritual than Biblical scholarship. There is no need to denigrate study of God's word in order to elevate the knowledge of God. This is a huge mistake. But unfortunately, this pastor goes much further.

"The devil knows and uses the Bible. The Bible in the hands of the Spirit is true. We need discernment to walk in the truth and to hear the Word of God, which brings life.....What did the devil use in the wilderness to try to destroy the Christ? The Scriptures! The most powerful weapon used against Christians is religion, and religion is the Bible without the Spirit.

---

[156] 2John 1:9

The Bible isn't always true. The Bible handled by the Spirit is true. The letter kills, but the Spirit gives life."

Again, I understand the point here but in order to strain out a gnat he has swallowed a camel. "The Bible is not always true." Unbelievable! Of course this is a flat out rejection of Scripture itself and its claims, whether he means it or not. The Bible is always true, regardless of how it is presented. Just because people use it in a wrong way, or teach it in a "religious" mindset, does not make it untrue. Jesus did not tell the devil he was lying because He wasn't, at least not this time. Jesus was being tempted to disobey the Father and use the Scripture to advance a different agenda, which He could have done. He did not respond with "That's not true because you are the devil." Rather, He responded with verses that revealed the evil agenda of satan and uncovered His selective usage of Scripture. Indeed, many so-called teachers are doing the same thing today. Furthermore, to say that "the Bible is not always true unless in the hands of the Spirit" is to place the authority of Scripture under the subjective feelings and whims of certain individuals. In other words, this pastor is telling us that unless anointed people like him, or those that he deems anointed, are handling the word it is not true. That is really arrogant! Furthermore, it is a frontal assault on the authority of Scripture. The Bible is the Word of God. It is already "God breathed" and does not need this pastor's "anointed" understanding or that of anyone else. Yet those who operate in what we call "the River" constantly make these kinds of statements. Evidently, they are unfamiliar with this verse:

"For the ***word of God (Logos not Rhema)*** *is living and active and sharper than any two-edged sword, and piercing as far as the division of soul and spirit, of both joints and marrow, and able to judge the thoughts and intentions of the heart." Heb 4:12 (Emphasis Mine)*

Dear friends the Bible is always right and is never subject to any person's interpretation. It does not need your anointing to be true – it already is. If you abuse its words for your own agenda or gain, you will bring swift condemnation and destruction on yourself. It is true that many misinterpret its teaching, but that does not make the Bible untrue or unreliable. It makes what those preachers say untrue and their ministries unreliable. It is true that we can unintentionally get a passage wrong or misunderstand, but that does not necessitate an assault on the accuracy of Scripture or a need to protect the Holy Spirit from His Word. I do not honor the Holy Spirit by dishonoring the written Word. But this sort of thing is now common among Revival ministers. Here is another popular quote:

"To value the scriptures above the Holy Spirit is idolatry. It is not Father, Son, and Holy Bible; it's the Holy Spirit. The Bible reveals God, but is itself not God. It does not contain Him. God is bigger than His book."

Again, there is an element of truth here, but it is dangerously overstated to pit the Holy Spirit against the book, or to separate one from the other. I do not believe that one who studies and truly loves the Scriptures will disregard the Holy Spirit any more than one who loves and submits to the Holy Spirit will disregard the written Word. Neither of these is optional. It is not the Father, Son and Holy Book without the Spirit. Neither is it Father, Son and Holy Spirit without the Book. Why not rather emphasize that we need the Holy Spirit and the Word and not sow a division between the two? Those who make these kinds of statements seem to like deliberately provoking people with their words to appear radically experiential, or "out of the box," as they say. This may appeal to the youth who generally dislike authority or what they deem to be "traditional" or "religious," but it may be sowing in them the seeds of rebellion. Thus, the study of Scripture and the need to handle it accurately is no longer a high priority among them.

You Report, Apostles Decide

Another point that needs to be made is that there seems to be a movement away from individual study of Scripture and Biblical accountability, to the pre-reformation days when the Bible was in the hands of an elite few. They alone were qualified to determine sound theology and the masses were expected to go along. Consider the following statement from a well know leader of the Apostolic Movement:

"What is theology anyway? Here is my attempt at a definition: Theology is a human attempt to explain God's Word and God's works in a reasonable and systematic way. This is not a traditional definition. For one thing, it considers God's works ***as one valid source of theological information.*** *For another, it sees God's Word as both what is written in the Bible (logos)* ***as well*** *as what God is currently revealing (rhea). Admittedly, a downside of viewing theology in this way is possible subjectivity, but the upside is more relevance to what the Spirit is currently saying to the churches on a practical level. Teachers research and expound the logos, prophets bring the rhema and* ***apostles put it together and point the direction into the future****." (Emphasis Mine)*

I wish I could say that this man's views were marginal but they are not. Indeed, because of his influence and others like him, they are finding their way into the mainstream. However, they send chills up and down my spine. What he is saying is that only the "apostles" or those that are deemed apostles and submit to certain "apostolic networks," have the right to form what is considered sound theology. Furthermore, he is saying that Biblical truth alone is not enough. Really? That's a shocker. Yet, the masses drink it like Kool-Aid. What does that say about their knowledge of the Bible? And what does it say about the direction these leaders are taking them? Dear pastor and Christian leader, isn't it time you woke up? Isn't it time to get back to reading the Bible again? Give the conferences a rest and shut yourself up with the

Holy Spirit and your Bible. It will save you a lot of money and your church will be better comforted knowing that you are a person who not only loves God but the Scriptures as well.

Prophetic Mayhem

One of the big problems in the Charismatic movement that has been undermining the Scriptures for decades, is the mayhem of the prophetic movement. Every day they parade out a new list of heavens declarations about nations and cities and the like, spinning the church with wild and even contradictory "visions" and "decrees." If even a tenth of their predictions were right, America and Europe and every other continent and island would be overrun by revival, undone by the power, fanatical in worship, and possessing the storehouses of Joseph and the treasuries of Cyrus. Indeed, every house in the Western Hemisphere would be equipped with a prayer tower, an eagle on the roof and a brand new wing for the prophet. Honestly, it is all very embarrassing. Let me say categorically that I love prophecy. I have a prophetic family and a prophetic class in our church that can prophesy with the best of them. But whatever happened to accountability and accuracy? While we were still waiting for the "saved and anointed" Bill Clinton to lead America, we were then told that Mitt Romney was now the chosen of God. Has there been an apology? No! There never is. They are already gone to the slick web page and the state of the art TV studio with the latest predictions. How exciting it all is! Furthermore, they have their own language – a sort of prophetic Christianese. And only those who know what "God is doing in the earth" understand it. However, before I get myself in more trouble than I am already in, let me get to the reason I brought this up. You see, this is the diet of the average Christian wanting to serve the Lord today. They are taught to use the Bible more like a diviner's rod than a measuring stick. They are taught to view it figuratively and allegorically rather than literally. The understanding of a passage is received from dreams, visions and angels, rather than a literal approach. They are taught that all passages have prophetic meanings and symbolic language. There is no one size fits all interpretation of anything. This is considered a "religious" approach. No one who is truly spiritual or "anointed" approaches the Bible like that or teaches like that. In addition, any passage can have almost any meaning as a "new revelation" is received. And while it looks God ordained and attractive to those who are wanting more, it undermines the authority of Scripture, by suggesting that the boundaries are all moveable, and there is no interpretation that can be locked in.

This was brought home to me years ago when an individual who was widely regarded as a prophetic teacher stood up in our pulpit and declared that the whole Bible was an allegory. I couldn't believe my ears. Needless to say, I did not invite him back. Yet, to my knowledge, he is still highly regarded as a teacher. I am not saying that these folks are being deliberately deceptive, or that there aren't any true prophets among them, but the movement as a whole is doing serious harm to the prophetic itself and undermining the authority and integrity of Scripture in the process. They are creating a whole generation of pseudo spiritual, hallucinatory Christians who know almost nothing about the Bible. Again, it is time for the church to wake up. It is time to hold prophets accountable for their words. It is time for those who are recognized as leaders to stand up and confront the obvious. Perhaps a fresh reading of 1Cor 14 would be in order.

The Bible According to Joe

Another culprit in the decline of Biblical knowledge and teaching is the overall flippant attitude toward the translation of the Bible itself and the consequent proliferation of pseudo Bibles. For centuries, hosts of scholars worked painstakingly with the original Hebrew and Greek Scriptures to give us the most accurate translations they could, even though some slight bias may have come through. Now every Joe can whip out his own version in his own words and call it the Holy Bible. And because the church is so ignorant, they don't even suspect anything. Once they see it online or hear some big name quote from it, they get a copy. "Oh this is so good," they exclaim. "I never heard it said like that before." That's because it never was. I am not suggesting that we should not have more translations of the Bible or that the KJV came down from heaven. I myself use the New American Standard Version (NASV) and occasionally the NIV. Incidentally, when I study I use the original and one does not have to be a scholar to do that. Anyone can consult an interlinear and there are many readily available online without any cost. There is no excuse for ignorance. However, in the last twenty years there has been a trend away from accuracy to modernity. It's no longer about sound doctrine but everyday language. This began somewhere in the seventies with the Living Bible put together by Kenneth Taylor. This was done primarily to put the Bible in a vernacular that children could understand. There is nothing necessarily wrong with this except for the fact that it is misleading to call it the Living Bible. The untaught and unsuspecting never know that it is not actually a translation of the Scriptures but Mr. Taylor's paraphrase. However, we have come a long way since the Living Bible came out. Now it seems as though "The Message" has become a standard among Evangelicals and Charismatics with many big names using it all the time. Again, there is nothing wrong with "The Message" per se, but it is not a translation of the Bible from the original languages. It is Eugene Peterson's paraphrase. It's the Bible according to Eugene. Again, though he means well and it has some good points, in many places it presents not only different words but also an entirely different meaning. I am not saying that Mr. Peterson is not qualified as a scholar; yet he does present his point of view. This is the reason that Bible translations were always put together by many scholars and to very specific guidelines, to be as accurate as possible to the original text and yet understandable to its readers. However, the trend now is toward modern vernacular and the language of the street, which in many cases waters down or changes the original meaning. Thus, it is the Bible according to Joe.

Besides that problem, there is also the reality that many of these companies, having been founded by Christians, are now owned by secular sources who wish to make money and be politically correct. This is why in some cases they keep updating their translations, so the Christian pastor and leader needs to be on his toes. In addition, some of the paraphrasers, so to speak, may be indulging themselves in the latest heresies and updating their works accordingly. I don't know about you, but I want to study the Bible according to the Holy Spirit and not the one written by Joe. Yet, many of the big ministries and ministry schools are quite happy to furnish their disciples with these works without ever explaining the difference. Furthermore, there is little focus on Bible scholarship in the current Revival Movement. This is a major problem that must be rectified if this generation of hungry believers is going to fulfill their call without shipwreck. There is ample evidence to suggest they are already in trouble, and those of my generation who are their mentors seem clueless that their dislike of sound theology is taking its toll. It's time to teach the Bible as it was written to the Hebrew people and educate God's people instead of continually apologizing for its difficult passages and watering them down. The Bible according to Joe may have its place, but make sure you tell them it's just Joe's version.

Church Schools

There was a time when a person who came to know the Lord and wanted to serve Him felt the need to go to Bible School. During the First Great Awakening for example, many Bible schools sprung up across the Northeastern United States. Though they were powerful in their day, sadly, most of these institutions are now secular liberal colleges at war with the Bible. Yet since that Great Awakening, and with each successive revival, many more Bible schools came into being, and some of them became renowned as Biblical learning centers. However, by the time of the Charismatic Movement in the 1960's Bible schools began to decline and for good reason. Though some have stayed true to the Word and the Spirit, over time Bible Schools tend to get overrun by those who do not have a personal relationship with God. The approach to the Bible becomes dry and intellectual and devoid of the Spirit. Many folks went to these institutions filled with faith only to come out without any. Others found Christ after they came out of these schools and seminaries and had to unlearn almost everything because they actually began to read the Bible. As a result, we tend to joke about them as cemeteries and learning the Bible began to be seen as more of an intellectual pursuit devoid of the Spirit. As a result, there came to be a perceived tension between the Spirit and the Word.

Another reason for the decline in Bible Schools is due to the curriculum, which was always affected by the beliefs or traditions of the founding denomination. Consequently, they tended to view the Bible through that prism rather than letting it speak for itself. This continues to be the norm with internet schools and institutes run by various networks. The candidate follows a carefully crafted curriculum, which consists of the agenda of the school based on the teachings of the founder or some extractions from Scripture, which may or may not be accurate. One can hardly consider it a careful study of the Bible or the whole counsel of God.

Over the last twenty years or so, many schools have sprung up in various churches and ministries, each with their own emphasis. They have mostly tended to focus on gifts of the Spirit and supernatural ministry or the Father's Heart. Though these schools have done much to prepare this generation through the healing of life's hurts and a hunger for the presence and love of God, they have done little to equip them in the word of God. It is not enough to teach people how to journal and prophecy and receive healing from the orphan spirit, though these are essential. The deception of Hyper Grace should make that very clear. The man or woman who would serve God and plant churches and spread the gospel around the world must receive an adequate training in the Scriptures from cover to cover and learn how to handle them accurately, while all the while growing and learning. We must raise up a generation of disciples who are burning with love for the presence of God and the truth of His Word. Nothing else is acceptable. Nothing else will last. If it is not founded upon the person of Christ Himself and the Words of His mouth, rather than the morsels of present or past revival celebrities, it is just wood hay and stubble that will be consumed in the fire.[157]

Conclusion

When I became a Christian in the mid 1970's, and began to read the Bible, I concluded that my training was to be in the local church. I studied the word of God on my own for nearly forty years and I have been to more seminars and conferences than you can imagine. I have been through two major world revivals in my lifetime and heard almost every imaginable spin. And though I do not have degrees after my name, I consider myself quite qualified to teach anyone who desires to learn. I am also a man of the Spirit and love His presence passionately. I give my time to training believers in the Bible from cover to cover. I believe in approaching the Bible from a Hebraic perspective, which is the way it was written. I did not arrive there totally on my own, but through the guidance of the Holy Spirit and direct and indirect mentoring of some fabulous Bible teachers over the years. I believe in taking the Scripture literally, unless the text itself suggests otherwise. My work may be slow compared to the progress of others, but I am certain of God's calling and choosing me.

Dear friend get back to reading the Bible yourself from cover to cover! Better still, make it a yearly habit. Read it without an

---

[157] 1Cor 3:`10-15

agenda, without helps, without commentary, and without headings. If you are too busy to do that then get an audio version that is an accurate translation and listen to it when you rise and when you drive. Meditate on it when you get up and when you lie down.[158] You will never be sorry. Instead, you may be surprised at how mighty and free you will become. I am not the slightest bit religious in the modern sense of the word, and have never used this expression in any church meeting. But I feel prompted by the Spirit to end this book with it.

May the Lord Bless the reading of His Word!

---

[158] Josh 1:8

Made in the USA
San Bernardino, CA
17 December 2016